The Disappearing American Farm

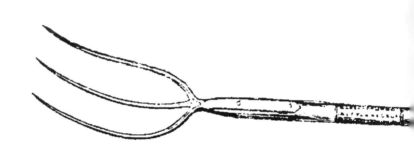

The
DISAPPEARING
American Farm

by Jake Goldberg

FRANKLIN WATTS *A Division of Grolier Publishing*
New York • London • Hong Kong • Sydney • Danbury, Connecticut

Cover photograph copyright ©: Landslides

Photographs copyright ©: The Pennsylvania State University College of
Agricultural Sciences: p. 6;
North Wind Picture Archives: pp. 27, 33, 34, 40, 44, 46; The Bettmann
Archive: pp. 31, 43, 77; UPI/Bettmann: pp. 61, 64; American Jersey Cattle
Association: p. 36; New York Public Library Picture Collection: pp. 37, 50,
54, 84; Ayshire Breeders Association: p. 106

Library of Congress Cataloging–in–Publication Data

Goldberg, Jake.
The disappearing American farm / by Jake Goldberg.
p.   cm.
Includes bibliographical references and index.
Summary: Describes the problems in American agriculture due to
technological innovation, gives a history of American agriculture to
explain the origins of the crisis, and outlines the limitations of
government farm programs and policies to cope.
ISBN 0-531-11261-6
1. Family farms—United States—Juvenile literature. 2. Agriculture—
Economic aspect—United States—Juvenile literature. [1. Farm life.
2. Agriculture.] I. Title.
HD1476.U5G65   1996
338.1'0973—dc20   95-49386   CIP   AC

CONTENTS

I

The *Farm Problem*

American farmers are without doubt the most successful and productive farmers in the world. They produce more food than Americans can eat, more than foreign nations can buy, more even than can be given away through aid programs and famine relief.

For more than one hundred years, since the closing of the frontier, American farmers, blessed with ample fertile land and an agreeable temperate climate, have succeeded through hard work, a willingness to innovate, revolutions in machine and biotechnology, and, most of all, the knowledge that the land is their own and that through their own labors they can truly improve their lives. American agriculture is based on the *family farm* system, on the principle that farmers shall own and live on their land and profit from the work they put into it.

When colonial settlers from Switzerland and Germany were establishing these independent, self-sufficient family farms in Pennsylvania in the seventeenth century, most farmers in other parts of the world worked as peasants, serfs, landless tenants, or even slaves—their labor enriching only their lords and masters. The independent farmer was a radical departure from tradition.

The independent family-owned and -operated farm lies at the heart of our idea of egalitarianism and has made a major contribution to the strength of American democracy. It has also given farmers an incentive to work hard, apply the latest techniques, improve their productivity, and outproduce all other farmers everywhere in the world.

In 1798 the English economist Thomas Malthus, looking at the crowded slums of London, put forth the grim theory that no matter how rapidly industrial societies increased the food supply, populations would always grow more rapidly, putting a strain on available resources and creating a permanent class of poor and hungry people. Only starvation and war, Malthus said, could bring food and population back into balance. Nowhere has Malthus been proved more abundantly wrong than in the United States, where for a hundred years farmers have continually outproduced the food demands of the population. This has guaranteed Americans a cheap and abundant supply of food that has been an underappreciated pillar of our economic growth and political stability.

According to the fall 1987 issue of the *National Food Review*, published by the Economic Research Service of the U.S. Department of Agriculture, in that year Americans spent 11 percent of their personal income on food. The French spent 17.9 percent of their income on food, the Japanese 19.9 percent, the Russians 25.6 percent, the Bolivians 35.5 percent, and the Nigerians 61.6 percent. Inexpensive and plentiful food is nothing to take for granted in this world.

Most of us would think that so much food is a good thing, but farmers are worried. Their very success in producing mountains of grain has driven down farm prices. Whenever there is more of something available than people want to buy, sellers reduce their prices as they compete to sell as much as possible in a glutted market. American farmers have been so successful in producing so much food that they have driven down the prices they receive, in many cases, below their cost of production. For many farmers, the reward for hard work, efficient management, and high productivity will be a lower income. This is the farm problem.

Wheat prices were holding steady at a respectable $3.50 a bushel in 1995. (A bushel is slightly more than 0.35 hectoliter [hl], or 35 liters.) A four-year drought in Australia has ruined one of our major competitors in wheat in international markets, and the shortfall of Australian grain has maintained worldwide demand for American wheat. But soybean prices fell to $5.40 a bushel, down almost $1.00 from last year, and corn prices fell below $2.00 for the first time in two years.

Low farm prices may help consumers save $6 billion on their food bills, economists say. Of course, consumers will not see the price of food decline. The price of food will actually rise by 2 or 3 percent in 1996. The prices paid to farmers by food processors never account for more than 25 percent of the retail prices of food. The cost of corn as a raw material accounts for no more than 5 percent of the price of a box of cornflakes. So food prices will rise because of higher transportation and packaging costs, but they will not rise as much as they might have if our farmers had failed us.

Caught between unpredictable and frequently low prices and the rising cost of operating a modern, efficient commercial farming operation, many farm families find that their income varies widely from year to year and is usually less than that of other workers. As a result, many farmers are deep in debt and thousands leave farming every year. Their land is absorbed into larger farms or turned into highways, shopping malls, or residential housing. A traditional way of life is disappearing, and there is a growing concentration of ownership in our food production system. This also is the farm problem.

To stabilize farm prices and farm incomes and to protect the hard-pressed farm family from bankruptcy, the government has developed a complicated entitlement program, a set of laws renewed or revised by Congress about every five years, known collectively as the "farm program."

Since the 1930s the government farm program has sought to protect farmers from low market prices with a complex program of *price supports*. The government establishes *target prices* for different crops, prices the government thinks are fair and will enable farmers to cover their costs of production. (This program is explained in detail in chapter four.) If farmers are offered prices lower than target prices in the marketplace, the government, through a complicated system of cash payments and nonrecoverable loans, pays farmers the difference between the low market price and the target price.

In earlier periods the cost of federal subsidies to farmers was a modest $3 or $4 billion. But in 1987, as farmers were just beginning to recover from another period of overproduction, shrinking demand, low prices, and high debt, the cost of the farm program to taxpayers reached a record $26 billion. Ever since that time, Congress has demanded reductions in target prices to reduce the cost of the farm program and to appease a growing number of critics of the program, which has become the third largest entitlement program after Social Security and Medicare.

This is an awesome burden for taxpayers, and in recent years it has generated a fierce debate over the appropriateness of this huge "welfare" system for farmers. This too is the farm problem.

With record 1994 harvests driving the price of corn down to $2.00 a bushel, with the federal target price set at $2.75 a bushel, the government may have to pay farmers 75 cents a bushel for a good portion of the more than 10 billion bushels (3.5 billion hl) of corn they grew this year. The Department of Agriculture estimates that the cost of the farm program will rise from $9 billion in 1994 to $13 billion in 1995. How will consumers compare their low food prices to what they lose as taxpayers in subsidizing farmers' incomes? How will politicians, in a time of concern over federal spending in general, respond to the increasing cost of this program? Already, in October 1994, President Clinton signed into law a reorganization of the Department of Agriculture that will shut down 1,274, or nearly one-third, of its field offices, ultimately eliminating 11,000 jobs. Farmers are beginning to feel that they have fewer and fewer friends in Washington, and they wonder anxiously how they will cope with low market prices if the farm program is scaled back or eliminated.

Who are America's farmers, and why are they in this situation? To answer the first question, on November 10, 1994, *The New York Times* reported new figures released by the Census Bureau showing that just under 5 million people, or less than 2 percent of the population, worked on 1,925,300 farms. This is the lowest number of farms in the country since before the Civil War. More than 70 percent of the total number of farms, about 1.5 million, are small farms earning less than $40,000 a year in gross income. These farms produce less than 15 percent of total farm output. They are too small to be profitable, and their owners all earn more from off-farm income than they do from farming. Into this category would fall the Iowa corn farmer with insufficient land and equipment to support his family, who works part-time as a manager of someone else's farm or who takes part-time work in a machine shop in town. Here too would be the farmer who tends that roadside vegetable stand or apple orchard and who, in the off-season, runs a small auto repair shop or takes a job in a local factory. The 1.1 million farms with gross sales from farming of less than $10,000, for example, have average total incomes of $22,000, the difference being attributable to non-farm earnings.

The government classifies as a farm any enterprise that earns more than $1,000 a year from the sale of farm products. Technically, an individual could sell one thoroughbred racehorse and be considered a

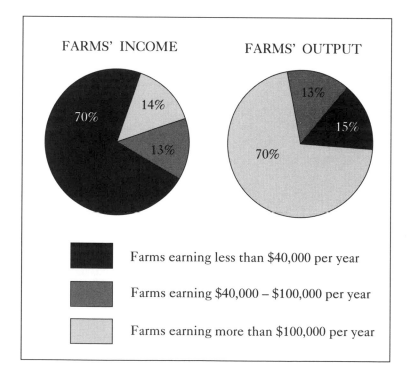

FARMS' INCOME

70%

14%

13%

FARMS' OUTPUT

13%

15%

70%

Farms earning less than $40,000 per year

Farms earning $40,000 – $100,000 per year

Farms earning more than $100,000 per year

farmer. And there are investors who purchase small, unprofitable farms to declare losses on their tax returns. But many of these smaller farms are run by true farmers whose limited resources force them to take on a second, non–farm job, just as many non-farmworkers do. Nevertheless, because these farms earn less from farming than from other sources, economists refer to them as money-losing "hobby farms" or "rural residences," and regard them as economically irrelevant.

If all such farms were to go out of business tomorrow, Americans would still have a surplus of food, but the character of life in many rural communities would change and thousands of small businesses serving these farmers would disappear along with them. Since many of these small farms lie close to urban and suburban areas, their disappearance would also further isolate city residents from farmers as urban greenmarkets closed and roadside farms were replaced by more gas stations and housing developments.

At the other extreme are perhaps 200,000 farms, about 14 percent of the total number, each with gross sales of more than $100,000. These farms produce about 70 percent of total farm output. About 100,000 of them have a gross income of more than $250,000, and about 30,000 of them earn more than $500,000 annually. Within this group of 200,000 farms can be found the large corporate farms and the family-owned "superfarms" that are really too large and require too much hired labor to be considered family farms in the traditional sense. Typical of the large corporate farm would be Tenneco West Inc., which owns a million acres (almost 405,000 ha) in California's Central Valley. (An acre is sightly more than 0.4 hectare, ha. A hectare equals 10,000 square meters.) Most of these superfarms are also run by farm families, using hired labor and highly efficient farming methods on thousands of acres of land. The 3,500-acre (1,400-ha) California vineyard owned by Ernest and Julio Gallo, which produces a third of all the wine consumed in the United States, is considered a family farm. All these farms are large-scale commercial operations with millions of dollars invested in land, buildings, and machinery. They take a disproportionate share of federal farm subsidies because of their size, but most would be profitable operations without these subsidies.

The remaining group—about 280,000 farms—constitutes about 13 percent of the total number of farms, with gross sales of between $40,000 and $100,000, and assets in land and equipment of no more than about $1 million. These farms generally fit the description of the traditional family farm, worked for the most part with family labor, though most of them are large-scale, highly mechanized commercial operations. These farms supply about 14 percent of total farm output. They are large enough to require the full-time labor of the farm family plus some seasonal hired labor, but they are not large enough to earn for their owners an income comparable to the national average. In 1987 the median national income was $30,853, but farmers in this middle group had a median income of only $18,713.

Most of the nation's food is produced by about 600,000 large and middle-size farms. If we count the farms that earn $40,000 to $100,000 in gross income, and if we then add a number of the smaller family-owned superfarms and some of the larger part-time farms, we get about 600,000 farms that together make up the core of the nation's family farm system. About one-third of the farmers in this group are in financial trouble. They cannot cover their production costs and are almost always in debt. Many survive only because of federal loans and price supports. It is the fate of this group of family farmers that has generated such heated debate in recent years.

A large number of small and middle-size family farms still survive as commercial operations. The family farmer is not about to disappear, but he may become economically powerless. Superfarms with sales of more than $200,000—less than 5 percent of America's farms—produce about 50 percent of our food supply. Many of the smaller family farms have surrendered much of their independence, as they produce under contract for food processing conglomerates, supermarket chains, grain merchants, and regional marketing cooperatives. Functioning less like independent farmers than like grower-subcontractors for larger businesses, many farmers no longer even make their own decisions about what to plant.

II

The Business of Farming

Where are America's farmers? Increasingly, American agricultural crops are becoming concentrated in specific regions of the country. Wheat production spreads over a vast area of the Midwest, but most of the big commercial wheat farmers are located in six states: Kansas, North Dakota, Oklahoma, Texas, Montana, and Washington. Kansas produces more than 22 percent of the total wheat harvest. The corn belt is centered in five states: Iowa, Illinois, Nebraska, Indiana, and Minnesota, with Iowa producing more than 20 percent of the total corn crop. Rice has traditionally been grown in Arkansas, Louisiana, Texas, and Mississippi, but California is now a major rice-growing state. Soybeans are grown in Illinois and Iowa, the two big corn- and hog-raising states. California and Florida are leading producers of vegetables and citrus fruits. Potatoes are grown in different regions, from Maine to New York State to Idaho. Cotton, tobacco, and sugar are grown in the southern states, peanuts in Georgia, and milk and dairy products in New England, the mid-Atlantic states, and Wisconsin.

The importance of agriculture to our economy should not be underestimated. In 1988 agriculture accounted for $170 billion, or 20 percent of the gross national product. In the same year, the export of farm products earned $36 billion, or 10 percent of all the nation's export revenues. Though there are relatively few farmers, millions of others who work in the transport industry, in food processing plants, supermarkets, and groceries, and in factories making tractors, combines, fertilizers, and pesticides are dependent on the farm sector to support them. In fact, one-fifth of the nation's labor force is involved in one way or another with our food production system.

The farm family today is no longer the isolated, stalwart, independent, and self-sufficient family of legend, and arguably hasn't been so since before the Civil War. The farm today is a commercial enterprise that must turn a profit to survive, and a farm that is large enough and well enough equipped to do that requires the full-time labor of adult family members as well as specialization in just a few crops. The modern wheat or corn farmer has no time to tend an orchard or a vegetable garden, or to raise dairy cows or chickens. Modern farm families lack the time and skills to make their own furniture, churn their own butter, and weave their own cloth, as they did in the distant past. The modern farm family shops for the things it doesn't grow or make for itself, just as urban families do.

The modern farmer is also dependent on the products and services of a complex industrial society. He no longer collects his own seeds but buys special hybridized varieties from seed companies. Tractors and planting and harvesting machines are supplied by a handful of large manufacturers, and the gasoline to run them is supplied by the oil companies. Antibiotics for animals are supplied by pharmaceutical firms, and fertilizers, insecticides, and weed killers come from petrochemical factories (see page 114). All this requires a lot of money, which the farmer does not have until he sells his harvest, and so he is dependent on the local banker for credit. The family farmer today is involved in a complex network of relationships to suppliers that has been labeled an *agribusiness* system.

As a consequence, the modern farmer hardly fits the urban stereotype of the rube, or hayseed, if he ever did. In addition to the traditional skills of farming—soil management, pest control, and knowledge of the weather—today's farmer must know a good deal about plant genetics, agrochemistry, the repair of complex machinery, and electrical and hydraulic engineering, not to mention cost accounting, business management, and the commodities markets and how distant economic and political events might affect those markets. Farmers today purchase more personal computers than any other occupational group.

What makes the family farm different from other businesses? Farmers, both as buyers and as sellers, are subject to forces outside their control. They cannot control their production with the same precision as, say, the industrial manufacturer. Floods, droughts, hail, frost, insects, and plant blights all play havoc with the size of a farmer's harvest, for farming, unlike manufacturing, is still bound to the rhythms and fickleness of nature. From year to year it is impossible for farmers or anyone else to know how much they will produce.

Because of this, farmers have no way of knowing how large the surplus will be in any year, what price they will receive in the marketplace, how much they will earn, or whether they have made wise or poor decisions in paying so much for seed and fertilizer and machinery.

As sellers of agricultural products, farmers operate in what economists consider a near-perfect model of a competitive free market. Whereas only a half dozen domestic and foreign automobile manufacturers control most production and can therefore influence prices, the farmer faces hundreds of thousands of competitors, all of whom are trying to sell the same kinds of products, and no individual farmer controls enough of the market to demand a particular price. All farmers are forced to sell at prevailing market prices, which remain low because of surplus production. No farmer can hoard his harvest until scarcity forces prices up, because other farmers will undersell him. Furthermore, because he does not know how much his harvest will earn, each individual farmer has to maximize production, to grow as much as he can, in order to earn as much as possible, whatever market prices are. Individual farmers are driven to increase their yields, even knowing that a larger aggregate yield will create a larger surplus and drive down prices even more. Thus the supply of food increases when it should decrease.

Yet the demand for food is described by economists as "inelastic," meaning that it does not vary greatly in spite of changes in supply and price. Americans consume about 1,400 pounds (635 kg) of food a year. As incomes improve, people make substitutions in their diet and consume more-expensive and higher-energy foods, often increasing their consumption of meat. But there are biological limits on how much food people can eat, and even if the price of food were to fall by 50 percent, Americans could not double their food consumption. People would not start eating four or five meals a day simply because food became cheaper. Even if all of the poor were provided with the diet and caloric intake of the rich, the total demand for food would hardly make a dent in agricultural surpluses. The rate of increase in food consumption cannot really exceed the rate of population increase, which in the United States has been quite modest over the past several decades. Nor can the farmer, like the manufacturer, increase the demand for food by growing a better or more useful product. Wheat, corn, rice, and other grains are called *fungible* commodities—that is, within certain grades of quality, one batch of grain is interchangeable with another.

Furthermore, most farmers do not sell directly to millions of consumers, or even to the tens of thousands of retail merchants who serve them. They sell to grain-elevator operators who negotiate prices through the commodities pits at the Chicago Board of Trade and at other commodities markets, where merchants, traders, food processors, and food shippers offer futures contracts, promissory notes to buy a certain quantity of grain at a certain price at a future time. Food conglomerates such as Pillsbury, Allied Mills, Archer Daniels Midland, Del Monte, and United Brands are large and powerful enough to demand that farmers accept the prices they offer. Only five large transnational grain-trading corporations—Cargill, Inc., the Continental Grain Company, the Louis Dreyfus Company, Georges André, and the Bunge Corporation—control virtually all of America's agricultural export trade as well as much of the world trade in grain. So the farmer, as one of hundreds of thousands of sellers, is confronted in the marketplace with a relatively small number of powerful buyers who, through their purchasing decisions, can have a great influence on farm prices. A situation in which many sellers confront just a few buyers is bound to drive down prices.

When manufacturers face a glutted market, they can slow down production, reduce their orders for raw materials, lay off workers, close factories, or even retool to make a different product. Farmers have none of these options. There are few production decisions they can make after planting. They cannot fire their own family, and their land and capital—tractors, combines, silos—have little use outside agriculture. For these reasons, economists say that the farm sector suffers from *immobility of resources*. Short of complete failure, farmers cannot reduce their costs, so they have no option but to continue growing as much as they can. As Lauren Soth writes in *An Embarrassment of Plenty,* "The theory of the market—that production will decline in response to a reduction in prices—simply does not work out. The 'automatic regulator' of free-market theory does not regulate agricultural production downward in a modern industrial economy—only upward."

So both as buyer and seller, the modern farmer has lost much of his economic independence to forces outside his control, and much more than other workers, who at least have a steady, dependable income, the modern farmer is fully at the mercy of the cash economy. The modern farm family faces a level of anxiety about its future that most non–farm families would find unacceptable. Just imagine what it would be like if urban office and factory workers were not paid until the end of the year, and had to borrow money to pay rent, food bills, and monthly expenses. Then suppose that at the end of each year, deep in debt, these workers found that their annual salaries were totally unpredictable and varied widely from year to year, sometimes covering their debts and sometimes not. Salaries would be unpredictable, but in general workers would discover that the harder they worked and the more they produced, the lower their hourly wage. Urban workers would then be in the situation faced by farmers.

If prosperity is elusive, the farm family does retain its traditional values: honesty, patience, and hard work, a reverence for the forces of nature and the sustaining power of the land, the sense of independence and equal status with others that comes from owning one's own land, and a sense of continuity with the generations that comes from raising children on that land. These values will be lost, some critics say, if the nation can't find a solution to the farm problem, if we can't devise an agricultural system that provides the family farmer with a stable and adequate income.

It is important not to lose sight of the peculiar context of America's farm problem. American farmers, as farmers if not as business owners, represent a success story. The farm problem, remember, would never have arisen if the land had been poor, if the climate had been unfavorable, or if farmers had been lazy or unwilling to innovate. Had that been the case, there would be no surpluses, no low market prices, and no need for expensive government programs. Then, of course, food would be scarce and people would be hungry, and we would have a very different and much more frightening farm problem. Let's take a look at how the family farming system evolved in America and how farmers got themselves into this mess.

III

The *Evolution of American Farming*

The first farmers in America were, of course, the first Americans. The Indians of the Plains and the forests of the Northwest lived mostly by hunting and fishing, but the Indians of the Southwest and the eastern woodlands farmed. They grew beans, squash, pumpkins, potatoes, peanuts, tomatoes, tobacco, and most important of all, corn. Their crop was not like the corn we know today. It was a short, scruffy-looking plant, with ears only 2 or 3 inches (5–8 cm) long. But it was tough and it would grow almost anywhere, and its seeds—the sweet, juicy kernels on its ears—were highly nutritious. Mixed with beans, squash, and peppers, in the Indian dish we know as succotash, it provided Native Americans with a complete diet.

Corn is unusual in that it is a completely domesticated plant. Like the other important cereal grains—wheat and rice—it is a descendant of the wild grasses, but corn requires human tending to reproduce itself. If left alone, the leafy husks that enclose the seeds will never open, and the kernels will have a hard time separating from the cob and falling to the ground. If an entire ear falls, it will probably rot, and should a kernel find its way into the ground to germinate, it will probably be choked by weeds. With no people to husk and harvest the ears, thresh out the seed, and plant it, corn cannot reproduce. The corn needed the Indians as much as they needed the corn.

When the first English-speaking colonists arrived in America, they brought wheat to sustain themselves. Wheat has a higher protein content than other grains, and it is a resilient plant, very resistant to drought. That was, in fact, the problem. Wheat grows well in a dry climate with little rainfall. It can survive cold winters, and it really flourishes during a hot, dry summer. In the mild, humid climate of the Atlantic coast, wheat did not grow well at all, and the colonists starved. Starvation and disease took more than half of the one hundred *Mayflower* settlers during their first winter of 1621. It was the Indians' gift of corn that saved them. Today corn is still a major American crop, but 80 percent of the harvest is used as livestock feed. The colonial farmer, on the other hand, ate corn all the time. It was baked into breads, cakes, and puddings and boiled into a mush known as corn pone, and it was eaten day after day.

The Indians also taught the colonists about crop rotation to allow the soil to recover its vigor, and they showed the colonists how to fertilize their fields with dead fish. The colonists had brought with them iron axes and farming implements, and they began to clear the enormous forests that stretched westward as far as the Mississippi River. It was backbreaking work, felling trees and digging out stumps and roots. Farmers also had to devote a good deal of time to hunting and fishing for the first year or two, until a good crop came in. They lived in simple log or sod houses, and they had to make most of what they needed. They fought insects, birds, and the weather to save their harvest. Smallpox, diphtheria, measles, and even the common cold killed them off, and a simple farming or hunting accident could lead to a lethal infection. The life of the colonial farmer was marked by hard work and commitment.

24

Patterns began to emerge. In southern colonies such as Virginia, Maryland, and the Carolinas, an English gentleman could receive a large land grant from the king to grow tobacco for export back to the mother country. At first, the fields were worked by indentured servants. Many of these men and women, impoverished or dispossessed commoners or even convicts, made the journey to the New World with the promise that after several years of labor for their masters they too would be entitled to a plot of land of their own to farm. Conditions in the tobacco fields were harsh, and these young men and women burned with a desire to be independent. As soon as their term of servitude was up, they deserted the plantations and struck out on their own. Faced with a shortage of labor, the large planters looked south to the West Indies, where the Spanish, having worked many of the West Indian natives to death on their sugarcane plantations, were now importing slaves from Africa to work their fields. Southern planters also took up this practice, and slavery was soon an American institution. A new, cheap crop—the peanut—was introduced to feed the slaves. Originally from South America, it had been taken to Africa, and the slaves themselves brought it to America. From the Bantu word *nguba*, meaning "nut of the ground," came the American word *goober*, another name for the peanut. Other crops well suited to the plantation system appeared, including rice and indigo. Cotton was not yet an important crop, because the labor required to separate the seeds from the boll made it too expensive to harvest.

The enormous demand for tobacco in Europe caused vast tracts of land in the southern colonies to be converted to its production. This was the first instance of commercial agriculture in the Americas. But tobacco was hard on the soil, depleting it of nutri-

25

ents, and the planters had to put new land under cultivation in seven-year cycles.

The plantation system spread westward throughout the South. With so much available land and cheap labor, the southern planters had little incentive to improve their techniques, even shunning crop rotation and the use of natural fertilizers. Prosperous farmers put their wealth into new land and more slaves, or into colonnaded plantation mansions built in imitation of the homes of English lords. It was a slow, indolent, aristocratic way of life that soon came to be despised by the smaller southern landholders and the innovative Yankee farmers in the North.

An entirely different pattern of farming evolved in the North, a pattern that was to establish the foundations of American democracy. The colonists who came to New England and to the mid-Atlantic colonies of New York, Delaware, New Jersey, and Pennsylvania brought with them, more than anything else, a fierce hatred of the oppressive feudal system of land tenure that still prevailed in the Old World. In England and the rest of Europe, many farmers were still peasants, little better than serfs, working land owned by the aristocracy. Life was hard and their diet was poor. In England, the big estate holders controlled Parliament. To improve food production and to create pasturage for sheep to supply the new woolen mills, they passed acts of enclosure that impoverished small farmers and squatters and drove them off the land. The poorer colonists arrived in America believing that land ownership was the key to independence. They crossed the ocean not to build cities or to work in factories but to acquire land and to become independent, self-sufficient farmers. To maintain that independence, they would fight the Indians, the French, and eventually their own English masters.

*In the northern colonies the self-sufficient family
farms were owned by the farmers themselves,
and all family members worked on the farm.*

This unique system of independent farmers, never before seen anywhere else in the world, came into its own in southeastern Pennsylvania. William Penn was the son of an admiral to whom the English king, Charles II, owed a favor. In 1681, Charles granted Penn a vast tract of land extending almost 300 miles (almost 500 km) west of the Delaware River. The king, a supporter of the Protestant cause in Europe's religious wars, offered Penn Protestant refugees from Germany, Switzerland, and Holland as settlers for his new colony. Some of them came to be known as the Pennsylvania Dutch. Penn was a Quaker who opposed war and slavery, and he insisted that all who came to his colony would enjoy freedom of worship, a promise that earned him the contempt of many stiff-necked New England preachers. But the idea appealed to those who wished to escape the economic and religious oppression in Europe.

What made this new system of farming so unique? First of all, Penn rejected the plantation system with its slaves, the large estate with its indentured servants, and all other forms of serfdom and peonage. Pennsylvania's farms would be owned by the people who worked on them. This meant that the farms would be small—perhaps no more than 200 acres (about 80 ha), the size that one farm family could manage on its own with the techniques then available. But these farmers would reap the rewards of their own labor, and so they had every reason to improve their techniques and make their labor more productive. Unlike Europe, where farmers lived together in villages and dispersed into the surrounding fields during the workday, Pennsylvania farmers built their houses on their own land. That land was their home, and farming was their way of life as well as their livelihood. The wealth that these independent farms generated would not be expropriated by a nobleman or a landlord, but could be used by the farm family to improve the land or to pay taxes, by common consent, to a local government for common purposes. The American system of free public education for all citizens, which had never been tried before anywhere else in the world, was promoted and paid for by American farmers.

Away from the Atlantic coast, west of the new city of Philadelphia in the drier climate of the fertile Lancaster Plain, farmers could now grow wheat, oats, barley, rye, and corn. They introduced a system known as mixed farming, which combined agriculture with animal husbandry, the raising of livestock. They developed new systems of crop rotation to grow their own food and food for their horses, cattle, sheep, chickens, and pigs. The animals in turn provided manure to fertilize the fields. They worked hard to increase their harvests by growing soil-regenerating plants and selectively breeding their crops for greater size and nutritional value. Better crops meant more and stronger, healthier animals, which meant more fertilizer and draft power to improve the fields in a self-sustaining cycle. The farmers also designed a new type of barn to accommodate this mixed farming. This German, or Swiss, bank barn, the Holzsteiner, was usually pitched against a hill. It had two levels. Grain was threshed and stored on the upper level, and the lower level was used as a stable to feed and house the livestock. The barn was often painted bright red with a mixture of whey, lard, and blood. To protect the animals and to prevent them from eating the crops, the farmer enclosed his land with fences, hedges, or stone walls.

The mixing of crops and livestock made the Pennsylvania farm family, for the most part, self-sufficient. Farmers still depended on the local miller to grind their grain into meal and flour, and they bartered farm products at the general store for sugar, salt, gunpowder, and iron implements. Neighbors helped each other when a barn had to be raised. But in almost every other respect they supported themselves. The animals provided not only meat and milk and eggs but also wool for clothing and leather for shoes and saddles. Small gardens yielded some vegetables, and apple, peach, and cherry trees were common. Corn and wheat provided food for man and beast; barley could be brewed into beer, and rye was distilled into whiskey.

As farmers prospered, they started to sell their farm products to the growing cities in the East. Crude roads were built linking the Lancaster Plain to Philadelphia and Baltimore, and in the early 1700s blacksmiths and wheelwrights in the village of Conestoga constructed a sturdy new wagon to haul goods east. Shaped somewhat like a boat, the wagon bed sloped down from either end toward its center, keeping its loads stable as it rolled over the primitive roads. A white linen hood protected the freight from the elements. The body of the wagon was painted a bright blue and the large wheels a deep red. A team of six horses bred for strength and size could pull up to 3 or 4 tons of goods an average of 15 to 20 miles (24–32 km) a day in a Conestoga wagon.

Though commerce had now come to colonial farmers and they no longer suffered from extreme isolation, they still depended on their own labors, and their ownership of the land made them fiercely independent. There were some "aristocrats" in American farming—the owners of the large southern plantations, for example, and the Dutch patroons with their great estates in New York's Hudson Valley. But the

*The original Conestoga wagon was shaped
somewhat like a boat.*

vast majority of colonists were self-sufficient small
farmers who regarded one another as equals and who
were no one's serfs.

The British, of course, did not see things this
way. There were many causes of the American Revolution, but the oppression and harassment of the colonial farmer played a major role. Farmers had to sell

their wheat, wool, and tobacco to English merchants at depressed prices, and they had to buy farm equipment and manufactured goods from England at inflated prices, which were made even higher by arbitrary taxes. The farmers were also obstructed in their efforts to improve their farming methods by prohibitions on the importation of improved varieties of seeds and cattle. In 1763 the English king, George III, decided to prohibit settlement west of the Alleghenies, further incurring the wrath of farmers, who saw their source of cheap land cut off. As a consequence, when the War for Independence finally came in 1776, it was the small independent farmers who made up the bulk of the Continental Army and who stood most firmly behind the ideas of Jeffersonian democracy, the "left wing" of early American political philosophy. It was, incidentally, the Conestoga wagon that carried the supplies and provisions for the Continental Army. Soldiers of the Revolution were cheered as trains of these bright red, white, and blue wagons rolled into their winter camps, and these wagons may even have given us the colors of the American flag.

After the War for Independence, the westward movement of farmers began in earnest. The new American government was unable to pay the long-overdue wages of the veterans of the Continental Army, so instead it granted them land in newly opened territory beyond the Appalachian Mountains. Thousands of settlers began to stream westward. The first wagon trains left Massachusetts and Connecticut in 1787. They were made up of modified, smaller versions of the Conestoga wagon, and men and women from the fishing villages of Massachusetts called them "prairie schooners" after the fishing boats they had left behind. By 1810, more than a million people had settled west of the Appalachians.

The first settlers rode west in smaller modified versions of the Conestoga wagon. The settlers called them "prairie schooners" because the wagons reminded the settlers of boats.

The American system of self-sufficient, independently owned farms, known today as the *family farm* system, rapidly spread from Pennsylvania to New York, New Jersey, and westward into today's states of Ohio, Illinois, Indiana, and Iowa—called the corn belt—and then northwest into the dairy farm region of today's Michigan, Minnesota, and Wisconsin. The farms grew larger, the style of the barns changed, and the mix of crops and animals was altered as farmers

*In 1798, John Chapman, known as
Johnny Appleseed, began planting apple trees
in Ohio, Indiana, and Kentucky.*

produced more grain and meat for sale to the eastern cities. But the basic pattern of family-owned farms prevailed throughout the northern United States.

The farmers were helped by uniquely American visionaries like John Chapman, an intinerant preacher, who in 1798 began to travel through Ohio, Indiana, and Kentucky clearing small plots of land and planting apple trees for no other reason than to make them available to the pioneer communities, earning himself the name "Johnny Appleseed." Other individuals also began to realize the importance of collecting and disseminating the knowledge and experience gained by farmers, and in 1819 John Stuart Skinner began the tradition of American agricultural journalism by publishing the *American Farmer*.

Improved varieties of livestock were brought in from Europe, and in the early 1800s alfalfa was imported from Germany to improve animal fodder. In 1810, ten thousand merino sheep were imported from Spain. Holstein, Jersey, and Guernsey cows were used for dairy products, and Hereford and Angus breeds were used as beef cattle. Superior animals would grow and fatten more quickly and could be slaughtered more frequently, increasing the amount of meat in people's diets.

In the South, the plantation system and slavery also moved westward, aided by the invention of a Yankee mechanic. In 1793, Eli Whitney, a graduate of Yale University, devised a cotton engine, or "gin," powered by a horse or mule, which could effectively remove the little green seeds from the tough fibers of the cotton boll. Before the introduction of the gin, a farm laborer could remove the seeds from 50 pounds (23 kg) of cotton a day. Now, operating the cotton engine, one individual could clean 1,000 pounds (450 kg) of cotton a day. Suddenly it was profitable to grow

*The Jersey cow's milk is used for
several dairy products.*

*Whitney's cotton gin introduced a new period of
American agriculture, utilizing machine
technology to increase productivity.*

cotton, and southern farmers abandoned tobacco for
the new crop. Whitney opened a factory in New
Haven, Connecticut, in the same year and began to
sell his gins to southern planters. In 1794 the South
exported a little more than 1 million pounds (about
454,000 kg) of cotton, but by the next year it was
exporting over 6 million pounds (2.7 million kg), and
the plantation system would eventually extend
throughout the Deep South all the way to Texas.

Whitney's cotton gin signaled the beginning of a new phase of American agriculture, the use of machine technology to increase farm productivity, but Whitney wasn't finished yet. During the War of 1812, against the British, he became interested in firearms. The early colonial musket was mechanically fragile and unreliable. It would frequently misfire. Its parts were crafted by hand and made for each individual musket. If a part broke or became misaligned, the whole musket was useless. Whitney devised a way to make musket parts from metal poured into molds and then trimmed and polished to standard dimensions. The parts were interchangeable, which meant that muskets built in this way could be mass-produced and easily and cheaply repaired. Not only had Whitney helped win the war against the British, but he had invented what came to be known as the American system of manufacturing, based on the mass production of standardized parts. This system was soon adopted by other arms makers—Colt, Winchester, and Remington—and it was also applied to the manufacture of farm implements, wagon parts, and just about any other kind of tool or machine Americans needed.

IV

The *Farms and the Industrial Revolution*

Eli Whitney had started America's Industrial Revolution, and over the next four decades thousands of factories began to appear in the cities and towns of New England and the mid-Atlantic states. A new class of industrial workers had to be fed. After 1815, railroads and steam-powered riverboats began to reach into the new farm communities, drawing East and West closer together and creating an incentive for farmers to become less diversified, to specialize in cash crops for sale to urban populations. At Washington Market in Manhattan, Faneuil Market in Boston, and Terminal Market in Philadelphia, urban merchants could buy fresh farm produce every day.

The westward expansion of the farmers was halted for a time when they reached Kansas and Nebraska and encountered the Great Plains. The Indians and the buffalo herds survived there, but for the farmers it was a terrifying sight. Suddenly there were no trees, and that meant no wood for houses, wagons, fences, or fuel. For a thousand miles (1,600 km), all the way to the Rocky Mountains, there was almost nothing but a vast level plain of shoulder-high prairie grass. Low areas were poorly drained and formed swamps and bogs where mosquitoes spread malaria. There wasn't much rain, but when it did come, it came in dark, towering thunderheads that boomed their way across the prairie, and with lightning bolts that started fast-moving wildfires in the thick grass. In summer, torna-

The handheld plow used in 1776

does scythed their way across the land, threatening to destroy everything a farmer might build. In winter, heavy snow covered the ground, and the plains became brutally cold. The first wagon trains to come this far passed through the prairie as through an awesome, uninhabitable desert—they didn't rest until they got to Oregon.

Some farmers noticed that the climate of the Great Plains was perfect for growing wheat and that underneath the prairie grass was rich black soil in which almost anything would grow. But to get at that earth, farmers would have to break up the hard topsoil with its tangled network of roots; otherwise, plowing would break the backs of their horses and oxen. It wasn't worth the effort. The problem was their plow.

The plow has been around for more than five thousand years, but for most of that time it was little more than a crudely carved wooden stick. The plow used by American farmers before the Civil War had a fairly advanced design. At the head of the plow was the coulter, a knifelike blade that made a vertical cut in the soil. Behind the coulter was the share, a horizontal wedge that cut and lifted free the strip of earth opened by the coulter. Attached to the share was a curved moldboard that lifted and curled over the strip of earth, exposing the underlying soil for planting. It worked well enough in the soft soil of the East, but it was made of cast iron and it simply wasn't strong enough for the plains. Plows broke or became hopelessly ensnared in the thick roots of the prairie grass, and the "sod" could not be "busted."

The problem was solved in 1837, when John Deere, a New England blacksmith who had settled in Grand Detour, Illinois, constructed a stronger and lighter plow from saw-quality steel. It cut through the tough roots easily without losing its edge, and it was self-scouring—that is, the hard topsoil of the prairie did not cling to the moldboard and foul the action of the plow. Deere formed a partnership with a sawmill owner, Leonard Andrus, and by 1846 he was selling one thousand of his new plows each year. He moved his company to Moline, Illinois, and by the mid-1850s was selling ten thousand plows a year.

With Deere's plow the vast prairie could finally be farmed efficiently. The Indians were driven out. The buffalo were slaughtered, and their hides were sent east to make leather drive belts for the new factories. The prairie grass was scythed or burned away, the marshes were drained, and the roots were plowed up to get at the rich subsoil. Because there was so much land, prairie farms grew in size. Instead of the 150- to 200-acre (60–80-ha) plots common in the East, farms on the Great Plains comprised 400 to 500 (160–200 ha) acres. Teams of four, six, or eight horses were soon pulling two, four, or six joined plows across the new large fields.

The farmers grew corn and oats for their animals, and wheat—endless acres of wheat—as a cash crop for shipment to the eastern cities and to Europe. As a result, the character of these farms began to change. The labor required to farm bigger plots and bring in large harvests of wheat gave farm families little extra time for the diversified farming activities that were practiced in the East. Horses provided essential draft power and had to be cared for properly, but other animals became a burden, and the system of mixed farming disappeared. Farmers put all their efforts into their one main cash crop—a system known as monoculture—and there were no resources to devote to the raising of cows, hogs, and chickens, the tending of gardens and orchards, and the dozens of other activities that had made the farm family more or less self-sufficient. The plains farm was evolving into a specialized commercial operation, and farmers were in a race to produce bumper harvests to earn the money for goods and services they no longer had time to provide for themselves.

New inventions eased the farmers' labor and increased their productivity. The old method of seed dispersal—broadcasting, or scattering the seed by hand across the fields—had always been inefficient. Now seed drills appeared that placed the seed directly into the ground in each furrow. Harvest time was especially critical. All crops are vulnerable to insects, birds, and other pests when they are ripe, and they are best harvested quickly. And the seed grains of wheat, unlike corn, will separate from the plant and scatter with the wind if they are not promptly gathered in. In 1831, Cyrus McCormick, the son of a Virginia blacksmith, invented a horse-pulled wheat harvesting machine that neatly cut the wheat stalks without scattering the grain. It also tied the stalks into shocks, compact cylindrical bundles that could be quickly gathered and threshed. In 1847, McCormick set up a factory in Chicago and in a few years was turning out a thousand of his mechanical reapers annually. In 1902,

*An Oregon wheat field is being prepared
for spring planting, circa 1880*

Cyrus McCormick's invention of a horse-pulled wheat harvesting machine—McCormick's reaper—further transformed American farming.

McCormick's company merged with its major competitors to form the International Harvester Company.

With the taming of the prairie, the westward expansion continued. Throughout the nineteenth century the frontier was settled at the rate of 30 miles (48 km) a year. Farms became larger and more mechanized, and after 1850 agricultural production soared. The Great Plains were destined to become one of the richest farming regions in the nation, often referred to as the "breadbasket of the world." The intensive cultivation and the resulting erosion of topsoil changed the ecology of the region, however. America's sparkling clear rivers turned brown as they filled up with silt, and the mighty Mississippi came to be known as the "Big Muddy."

Large commercial farms serviced by machines had a profound effect on the way farmers earned their living. Because these machines were expensive, as many as fifteen or twenty farmers would sometimes jointly purchase one reaper, and they would work together at harvest time. A good deal of cash was now needed before planting could begin, and farmers began to borrow money from a network of small banks that arose in western towns and cities. Farmers began to show concern for low interest rates and easy credit policies and what the national government would do to promote them. They became the driving force behind political populism, the movement to fight the tight credit policies and the domination of the economy by powerful eastern bankers.

Though their way of life was changing and western farmers were no longer quite so self-sufficient, they were still staunchly independent in their thinking. In the 1850s they were Free-Soilers and Republicans, and when the Civil War began, their sons joined the Union Army to prevent the plantation owners from turning the new territories into slave states. With their sons in the army and the farm family's labor supply reduced, farmers became even more dependent on their machines.

During the Civil War the Department of Agriculture was established. It began to publish information on the output of American farmers. It tested farm machinery and analyzed soils, and it gave out to farmers new plants and improved varieties of seeds. Congress passed the Homestead Act during the war, granting 160-acre (65-ha) plots in the West to anyone who would settle there, and the Morrill Act, which gave large grants of federal land to the states if from the proceeds of the sale of the land the states would build agricultural colleges.

With the abolition of slavery, the southern planters lost their labor force, but they were reluctant

The Texas longhorn—the beef cattle of the western ranches—became part of the food production industry in the mid-nineteenth century.

to sell their land to their former slaves. A system of sharecropping arose, whereby free blacks would work small parcels of the planter's land in exchange for a portion of the profits of the cotton harvest. Former plantation owners divided their land into 40- or 60-acre (16- or 24-ha) plots and assigned them to their tenants. By the turn of the century, free blacks were working almost 15 million acres (6 million ha) of land. Sharecropping was a harsh system that offered little opportunity to become truly independent, however, and the number of black farmers in the South soon began to decline as blacks migrated to northern cities and mechanization came to the cotton fields.

In the southwestern United States there was insufficient rainfall to support the kind of farming that took hold in the North, but there was ample land covered with scrub grass and brush suitable for grazing cattle. The settlers took over and developed the ranch system created by the Spanish and Mexicans before them and concentrated on raising livestock. Young men were hired to go out and round up the Texas longhorns, descendants of the first cattle imported by the Spanish, which now roamed wild. Unlike the Hereford and Angus breeds raised on the eastern farms, the Texas longhorns could feed exclusively on wild grass in a region where corn and other animal feeds were difficult to grow. The cattle were fattened and then driven in great herds from Texas ranches to railheads in Kansas, and the legend of the cowboy was born. Beef cattle and railroads created the city of Chicago, which by the 1850s was a sprawling complex of slaughterhouses, meatpackers, wholesalers, millers, and toolmakers. The city's bankers and speculators controlled the price of cattle, hogs, corn, and wheat. In 1854 the first beef from western ranches appeared in New York's markets.

By the 1870s the frontier had all but disappeared and almost the entire United States had been settled. In California, during the Gold Rush in 1848, John Bidwell, a farmer who had come west from Missouri, struck it rich in the gold fields north of Sacramento. But gold mining wasn't his real interest. He sold his claim and established the Rancho El Chico, where he grew apples, peaches, plums, raisins, olives, nuts, and—until he joined the temperance movement—grapes for wine. He proved that California's warm, frost-free climate was ideal for growing fruits and vegetables. Soon, with the help of Asian immigrants, who provided cheap agricultural labor, farmers transformed California's deserts and marshes into the richest fruit- and vegetable-growing region in the nation.

The country was also in the midst of a transportation and merchandizing revolution. New settlers were now coming west by railroad rather than by wagon train, and two Chicago meatpackers, Philip Armour and Gustavus Swift, began using refrigerated railroad cars to ship sides of beef back east, eliminating all the costs associated with transporting live cattle. The packaging and preserving of food also made great strides. In the early nineteenth century the French baker Nicholas Appert had successfully preserved vegetables for Napoleon's armies by boiling them and sealing them in glass bottles with waxed corks. The British improved upon the technique by sealing food in tin canisters, and in the 1840s William Underwood, an Englishman who had settled in Boston, established the first American canning factory for pickles, jellies, and jams. In 1848, Nathan Winslow of Portland, Maine, began to can sweet corn for New England's whaling fleets, and in 1860 Thomas Duckwell of Ohio began marketing canned tomatoes.

In the 1850s, Gail Borden of Texas mixed strips of beef with cornmeal and milk and placed the mix in a food dryer, to produce a hard, dry biscuit that would not rot and which provided food for western settlers and occupants of army posts. He traveled to England, where Borden Beef Biscuits won an award at a London exhibition. On the sea voyage home, Borden looked with concern at the poor immigrants crammed into steerage, knowing that many would soon die from malnutrition and disease as they packed themselves into city tenements or made the long trek westward to begin new lives. He saw the obvious need for a cheap, nutritious food that would not spoil. Upon his return, he went to Lebanon, New York, where Shaker farmers were experimenting with the preservation of foods and vegetable seeds. By 1853 he had perfected a process for making condensed milk, the only kind of milk that could be safely consumed before pasteurization, and in 1856 he established a canning factory for the new product in Passaic, New Jersey.

Other technical and scientific innovations promoted the growth of American farming. In the 1840s, German and English chemists discovered that nitrogen in the soil stimulated plant growth, and the first factories producing artificial fertilizer appeared in Boston and Baltimore in the 1850s. Hundreds of thousands of tons of guano, nitrogen-rich bird excrement, were imported from Peru to restore the soil of the southern cotton fields. New farm machinery was developed that would thresh grain, separating the seeds from the chaff. In 1865, the Austrian monk Gregor Mendel announced his discovery of the principles of inherited genetic traits, and the selective breeding of improved plants and animals was put on a scientific basis. In the 1870s, the problem midwestern farmers had in fencing their land in a region lacking wood was solved when Joe Glidden and Jabor Haish of Illinois invented barbed wire.

From the 1870s until the 1920s, American farmers experienced a period of unprecedented growth, change, and general prosperity. Hundreds of thousands of immigrants from Scandinavia, Germany, Ireland, Italy, England, Mexico, and Asia poured into the country to work in factories, to build railroads, and to farm. In 1870 there were fewer than three million farms in the United States; by 1900 there were more than five million farms; and by 1920 almost six and a

The replacement of animal power by machine power increased farm productivity enormously.

half million. By 1916 the amount of land under cultivation in the United States had doubled to more than 800 million acres (about 324 million ha). In 1870 the average farmer produced enough food to feed about five people, hardly more than the number of people in the average farm family. By 1920 farm productivity had increased to the point where the average farmer's surplus could feed ten people. By the turn of the century almost 240 million bushels (85 million hl) of wheat—about one-third of the total harvest—had become available for export to foreign countries, earning America vital foreign exchange and promoting economic development.

In addition to the new land put under cultivation, there were continuous improvements in farm machinery. Better plows, grain drills, harvesters, and threshers were complemented by new manure spreaders, mechanical pickers, hay loaders, milking machines, and cream separators. By the 1870s some farm machinery was being powered by steam engines, and by the 1920s crude gasoline-powered tractors were pulling the cultivators and harvesters. A remarkable transformation occurred during World War I and in the years afterward as farmers gave their horses and mules to the army or shipped them off to slaughterhouses while they converted their barns and stables into toolsheds and machine shops. Machine power was replacing animal power, with enormous consequences for farm productivity. In 1840 it had required over 230 man-hours of labor to produce 100 bushels of wheat; by 1900 it required only about 100 man-hours. Furthermore, the disappearance of the workhorse during the 1920s enabled farmers to convert 25 million acres (10 million ha) of land from growing animal fodder to growing food grains, making American agriculture even more productive in terms of food for people.

In spite of the general prosperity, however, American farmers were learning some hard lessons— first and foremost, that farming was now a business. Farmers were part of a cash economy, and if they did not earn enough from the sale of their crops to pay their expenses, they could lose everything, including their land. Farmers could no longer produce everything they needed on their own. Their time had become too precious and their labor too specialized. They were in debt to the banks for their purchases of land, machinery, fertilizer, and gasoline. As western farms grew bigger—and by 1900 many were more than a thousand acres—farmers needed cash to pay the wages of extra workers at harvest time. Farm families also wished to live as well as city folk, so they needed money for furniture, sewing machines, kerosene stoves, telephones, pianos, and all the other wonderful products of America's Industrial Revolution. To earn this money, farmers had to work the land for all it was worth. This was the beginning of a system of farming that Robert West Howard in *The Vanishing Land* characterized as "techno-serfdom." The independence of the family-owned and -operated farm was becoming precariously balanced between the market price per bushel of wheat or corn and the size of loan repayments to the bank, and if enough cash did not flow through the system, the land where generations had been raised might have to be forfeited to creditors.

Though the growth of cities provided farmers with the large markets they needed to match their increased productivity, the cities and their interests were becoming a problem for the farmers. By the 1880s, though the number of people in farming continued to grow, the number of people who lived in cities was greater. City dwellers were electing more and more representatives to Congress, and urban politics began to overshadow farm interests. Farm prosperity increasingly depended on the interest rates that banks charged for loans, on the freight rates charged by the railroads, and on the prices distant factories and refineries charged for machinery and fuel. When farmers tried to sell their agricultural products, they found that traders in Chicago set the prices for wheat, corn, and cattle. The prices for wool and lamb were set in Boston; the prices for poultry, milk, and dairy products in New York; cotton in the port cities of New Orleans and Savannah; and fruit and vegetables in San Francisco, Los Angeles, and Miami. Farmers were, in short, beginning to experience the "farm problem." They were being squeezed between the low prices their surpluses were causing and the high prices of everything they needed from the cities to continue farming. By 1889, though their harvests were 25 percent larger than they had been during the 1850s, wheat farmers were receiving 30 percent less income than they had received in 1881.

Farmers resisted this squeeze. In 1867, William Saunders, Oliver Kelley, and several other employees of the newly formed Department of Agriculture founded the National Grange Order for the Patrons of Husbandry, a secret society designed to help farmers. At first, membership in the Grange remained small as farmers reacted with suspicion or amusement to its Masonic-like rituals and secret passwords. But a financial panic in 1869 on the eve of the Franco-Prussian War drove the price of wheat down to half of its previous price while farmers' costs remained high. Something had to be done, and the Grange seemed to be the answer. Saunders and Kelley had been encouraged by a group of radical weavers in the English midlands who formed the Rochdale Cooperative. The weavers had pooled their resources to buy the food and equipment they needed at wholesale prices, and they sold their cloth directly to English tailors as a group, refusing to compete against one another, negotiating the best possible price, sharing the profits, and

As a response to the "farm problem," the National Grange Order for the Patrons of Husbandry was founded in 1867.

eliminating the middlemen. Saunders and Kelley advocated a similar nationwide system of cooperatives for American farmers, and the idea took hold.

By 1875 the Grange had 20,000 chapters in the United States and more than a million and a half members. They didn't always refer to themselves as members of the Grange; some called themselves Independents, Reformers, or Antimonopolists. But whatever they called themselves, farmers began to form cooperatives for the sale of wheat, corn, cattle, and hogs. With their savings, farm cooperatives were soon buying their own grain storage and milling facilities and their own feedlots and stockyards. Some chapters even sold farmers' life insurance, and others became interested in politics, electing national and state legislators who promised to fight for lower interest rates and lower railroad freight charges.

But the Grange could not compete against the growing power of the middlemen—the wholesalers and traders, the millers and food processors, the packagers, and the railroads—all of whom were adding their own services to the cost of food and rendering the farmers' contribution less and less important. By 1890 the Grange could claim hardly more than 100,000 members. Other farm organizations, alliances, and movements followed, though, and the cooperative movement remained strong in certain areas, especially among the fruit growers of California.

In the 1890s farmers joined with union workers to form the Populist Party. In 1896 and 1900, afraid that easy credit would dry up if the government printed only as much currency as it had gold in its vaults to back the currency up, farmers voted for the charismatic Democratic presidential candidate, William Jennings Bryan. Bryan, known as the "Great Commoner," had said, "You shall not crucify mankind upon a cross of gold." Bryan's defeat in those two elections by Republican William McKinley, and a third defeat in 1908 by Republican William Howard Taft, symbolized the irreversible decline of farmers' political power as a new industrialized and urbanized America entered the twentieth century.

In spite of rising costs and a loss of control over the economic environment in which they operated, farmers continued to prosper up until the end of World War I in 1918. The war devastated European agriculture, and American farmers put 40 million new acres (16 million ha) under cultivation to feed Europe's people and the Allied armies. Even with this increase in output, farm prices rose, and farmers referred to this period as the "silk shirt years" even as they became more dependent on the cash economy. When American soldiers went overseas in 1917, the shortage of labor forced farmers to double what they spent in wages for hired hands and to quadruple their investment in farm machinery. But in 1918 and 1919, in spite of rising costs and increasing indebtedness, farmers' income exceeded that of non-farmers by 50 percent.

During the 1920s American farmers began to experience hard times as they no longer found ready markets for their surpluses in foreign countries. Nations saddled with huge debts from the war found it difficult to continue paying for American grain, and with the armies no longer marching across the land, European agriculture began to recover and compete with American farmers in world markets. By 1928 even the newly formed Soviet Union was exporting wheat. And there were new competitors from nations that had not been ravaged by the war—Canada, Argentina, New Zealand, and Australia. Exports of American farm products declined, and the gross income of American farmers fell by $4 billion in 1920. Mechanization was increasing, and farmers continued to produce surpluses, driven by the need to maximize production to pay their rising costs, but the surpluses only drove down the market prices for their crops. Land purchases and investment in new machinery and equipment, made during the war years to increase production, had driven many farmers deeper into debt. Between 1910 and 1925 the value of mortgaged farmland rose from $3.3 billion to $9.4 billion. Droughts in the Midwest brought more hardship, and between 1920 and 1929 more than six million people left the farms to look for work in the cities. The race to work the land for all it was worth increased soil erosion, so that by the mid-1930s huge dust storms in Kansas, Nebraska, Oklahoma, and Texas ruined the land and darkened the skies as far east as Washington, D.C. A million people were uprooted by the dust storms, their farms destroyed, their land seized by the banks to pay their debts. Those farmers who didn't lose their land were just hanging on, producing more food than they could sell at a price that barely covered their costs. The plight of the farmers led the United States into the Great Depression, but it wasn't until the Depression became general after 1929 and began to affect urban workers that government found the political energy to offer relief.

V

The Government Steps In

The New Deal farm programs of the 1930s were not the first attempt by government to manage agricultural production. In 1916, during the administration of Woodrow Wilson in World War I, Congress had passed legislation to create privately owned, federally supported land banks to make easier credit available to farmers. With new loans, farmers were to purchase or lease new land and cultivate it to feed the war-torn nations of Europe. The government, through its U.S. Grain Corporation, also purchased agricultural products for export and guaranteed farmers a good price. But when the war in Europe ended and foreign demand for American farm products decreased, the land banks only contributed to a higher level of farm debt and greater crop surpluses, which drove down farmers' prices. Then, in 1920, the U.S. Grain Corporation stopped buying wheat, and the price fell by 50 percent.

Meanwhile, European agriculture had recovered and American farmers now had to compete in international markets against farmers in Canada, Argentina, and New Zealand. The instability of foreign markets and the threat of foreign competition led many politicians and some farmers to conclude that America should abandon foreign markets, curb output, produce only enough crops to feed itself, and stop importing competing foreign goods. From 1921 on, Congress passed increasingly severe tariffs—taxes on imports—culminating in the Smoot-Hawley Tariff Act of 1930, in an effort to reduce the number of foreign products sold in this country.

But tariffs can hurt a country in several ways. Other countries may retaliate against our exports by imposing tariffs of their own. Even if there is no formal retaliation, other countries, unable to sell in America, will not be able to earn the dollars to buy American goods, and American exports will decline for "natural" economic reasons without political retaliation. This is what now happened. In 1929, the year before the passage of the Smoot-Hawley Act, the United States had exported 40 percent of its wheat, 55 percent of its cotton, and more than 30 percent of its tobacco. In 1930 and 1931 those and other American exports declined by 50 percent. America's foreign trade collapsed, and the American farmer reached a point of desperation. Many economists believe that these restrictive tariffs and other protectionist measures by the United States and other countries turned a serious but manageable economic downtown into a major worldwide depression.

During the early years of the Great Depression, President Herbert Hoover urged farmers to reduce their harvests and abandon production for foreign markets. Hoover believed that the key to a fair price for farmers lay in the efforts of farm cooperatives, which could hold back from the market large quantities of grain, creating an artificial scarcity and driving up farm prices. In 1929 Hoover established a Farm Board with a budget of $500 million, the purpose of which was to make liberal loans available to farm cooperatives if they would agree to hold their products off the market. The government also set up a Grain Stabilization Corporation to buy up surplus farm goods that would ordinarily have been offered for sale in international markets. The expectation was that this artificially engendered scarcity would drive up the price of farm products and that, when the price was right, the cooperatives would put their stored crops on the market, reap a profit, and pay back the Farm Board loans.

At first the efforts of the Farm Board did produce modest increases in the price of farm products, if for no other reason than that the U.S. Grain Corporation was willing to buy grain from farmers at prices above those of the world market. But the Farm Board's $500 million budget was not nearly large enough to create a real scarcity. Everyone knew that huge surpluses of grain were accumulating in government and cooperative storehouses. Eventually these surpluses would have to come to market, so buyers refused to bid up the prices of farm products. By 1930 the prices of wheat and corn were dropping precipitately. And with the collapse of the export market, nothing could compensate the farmers for the loss of the sale of some 50 million bushels (18 million hl) of grain to foreign consumers, who now turned to other producers in Canada, Argentina, and New Zealand. The cooperatives were not strong enough to control the market. They could temporarily stockpile and refuse to sell their produce, but they could not curtail production. They could not limit the farmers' need and drive, especially in hard times, to increase their harvests, though this created the surpluses that drove down prices for all farmers. Nor had the government been wise enough to manipulate the grain trade to the advantage of farmers, having given away the foreign markets that might have raised their income. In fact, by 1932, total farm income in the United States had fallen more than 60 percent below the already low total for 1929, and many farmers

*Farmers listen as their land is auctioned to pay overdue
taxes in Spotsylvania, Virginia, in 1933.*

faced bankruptcy and foreclosure. The Hoover farm program had failed.

In 1933, Franklin D. Roosevelt assumed the presidency with a belief that government had to aggressively manage agricultural production to reduce surpluses and guarantee farmers the kind of prices and incomes that would keep them on their farms. He had stated during his campaign his belief that low farm income was at the root of the entire Depression. Roosevelt's farm policy was based on the concept of *parity,* a concept developed at the Department of Agriculture during the 1920s. Government would guarantee farmers a price for their products that gave them the same purchasing power they'd had during the prosperous period between 1910 and 1914, when their living standard was on a par with that of urban workers.*

Roosevelt appointed Henry A. Wallace as his secretary of agriculture. Wallace had been the editor, after his father, of an influential magazine, *Wallace's Farmer*. He had also developed a new strain of high-yield hybrid corn, which he sold through his own firm, the Pioneer Hi-Bred Corn Company. Wallace shared Roosevelt's views on agricultural reform and

* The Department of Agriculture developed a *parity index*, a number based on the prices farmers had to pay for more than three hundred products and services, including taxes, interest on loans, and the salaries of hired laborers. This index number might be a certain number of points above or below 100, depending on whether farmers' costs exceeded or fell below those of the 1910–1914 base period. An *index of prices received* by farmers was also developed, which compared changes in the prices of more than fifty agricultural products with prices during the same base period. Dividing the index of prices received by the parity index, the Department of Agriculture calculates the *parity ratio*, which reveals whether farm prices have been increasing or decreasing compared to farmers' costs. Dividing the unit price—per bushel, pound, or hundredweight—of a particular farm product during the 1910–1914 base period by the index of prices received for the base period, and then multiplying the result by the current parity index, will yield the parity price, the price a farmer should receive to have a real income comparable to that of the base period.

the need for quick, decisive government intervention to save struggling farmers.

According to the Department of Agriculture's parity calculations, the purchasing power of farmers in 1932 was only 55 percent of what it had been in 1910–1914. Farmers, who still made up nearly a third of the country's population, were angry. They destroyed milk trucks, picketed food processors, and in one instance nearly lynched a federal judge who was handling farm bankruptcies. John A. Simpson, president of the Farmers' Union, thought the situation so serious that he wrote to Roosevelt stating that "unless you call a special session of Congress . . . and start a revolution in government affairs there will be one started in the country. It is just a question of whether or not you get one started first."

To gain the authority the government needed to intervene in the nation's farm economy, in 1933 Roosevelt pushed through Congress the Agricultural Adjustment Act. Parts of the act were later declared unconstitutional by the Supreme Court, but with the revisions contained in the Soil Conservation and Domestic Allotment Act of 1936 and the second Agricultural Adjustment Act of 1938, Roosevelt overcame constitutional objections and established a comprehensive program of agricultural controls. Two important points must be made before we discuss these programs. First, all of the government programs were voluntary. Many farmers have never participated in government farm programs, though the programs themselves affect market conditions for all farmers and sometimes create strong economic pressures to participate. Second, though Wallace himself said that they were "admittedly but a temporary method of dealing with an emergency," the New Deal farm programs created a model for government management

Henry Wallace, President Roosevelt's secretary of agriculture, speaks to the conference of Associated Country Women of the World in 1936.

of agriculture that in one form or another has continued to the present day, with results that are hotly debated.

The problem, everyone seemed to agree, was surplus agricultural production. American farmers produced more food than American consumers could eat and more than foreign nations, hungry or not, could afford to buy. The surpluses depressed farm prices, so the new legislation was designed to raise farm prices by destroying the surpluses. The cruelest part of the government program involved the destruction of surplus crops by order of the secretary of agriculture. Large amounts of milk, dairy products, and food grains were disposed of or allowed to rot. Six million baby pigs were slaughtered, and 10 million acres (4 million ha) of cotton were plowed under. The destruction of food during an economic depression, when the poor and the unemployed were going hungry, seemed irrational and caused a great deal of outrage. Secretary Wallace carried out the destruction with great reluctance, but raising farm income was the priority and the surpluses had to be reduced.

Future agricultural surpluses would be controlled by three mechanisms: conservation subsidies, acreage allotments, and price supports. In conservation subsidies, the Department of Agriculture, through its newly established Agricultural Adjustment Agency, made cash payments directly to farmers who agreed to set aside a portion of their land from crop production and plant instead soil-conserving grasses and legumes. Farmers who reduced their production of food grains would receive an annual payment from the government in the name of soil conservation.

In acreage allotments, apart from whether or not soil-conserving crops were planted, the government established an additional acreage reduction program.

The Department of Agriculture made an annual estimate of how much food American farmers should produce for domestic consumption, for exports, and to provide an adequate reserve. A recommendation was then made for an overall reduction in the amount of land devoted to the cultivation of each major food crop. The Department of Agriculture calculated each farmer's base acreage—the average acreage planted during the previous five years—and then suggested that plantings for each farm be reduced by a specific number of acres. The general aim of the program was to subsidize farmers so as to create a greater scarcity of farm products. Early New Deal farm programs paid farmers directly for the acreage taken out of production and for acreage planted to soil-conserving crops. Those laws were later changed, however, and it is now technically incorrect to say that farmers are paid not to grow crops. Farmers no longer receive cash payments for compliance with acreage-reduction programs, but compliance is usually required if farmers want federal farm loans or the benefits of the third government program, price supports.

The price support system—a complicated set of calculations, was operated by a federally owned corporation, the Commodity Credit Corporation, which worked hand in hand with the Department of Agriculture. The farmers' purchasing power for the 1910–1914 period was the measure used to set parity. The government decided what level of parity it wanted to maintain, depending on the level of production it wanted to encourage. That level might be 50, 75, 90, or 100 percent of parity. The government then determined the parity price, or target price, for each crop. The target price was the price per bushel or pound that farmers should be paid to raise their real income and purchasing power to whatever percentage of the 1910–1914 level the government had mandated.

In more recent years, farm programs have abandoned the 1910–1914 base period as an unrealistic measure of current farm prosperity. Politicians have recognized that farm products, like manufactured products, *should* become cheaper over time in a healthy, growing economy with improved technology. Prices cannot be maintained at the levels of 1914, a period that could be called a pre-technological era in American farming. Current formulas for calculating parity prices are based on average farm prices for the preceding ten years. But the principle is the same: the government decides what prices farmers should receive for their crops in order to maintain their purchasing power at some predetermined level.

In most cases the price supports were applied indirectly through a *non-recourse loan*. The Commodity Credit Corporation established a *loan rate*— a price per bushel, pound, or hundredweight for various farm products. Using this price, it offered farmers a loan that was equivalent to the value of their crops after the harvest. Farm prices are usually low at harvest time when an abundance of products is brought to market. These non-recourse loans enabled farmers to hold their crops off the market until they could obtain a better market price. In this case, the collateral, the asset that backs up the loan, is the farmer's crop itself. The farmer has a choice: either sell the crop at a favorable market price and pay back the loan, or default on the loan and turn the crop over to the government, which will accept the crop instead of repayment. Farmers must observe trends in market prices and then decide whether or not to market their crops; for in order to obtain the loan, they must agree to forfeit the full crop upon which the amount of the loan is calculated, should they decide to default. Farmers have up to nine months after harvest time to decide to market their crops before the government takes it. The loan rates, it should be noted, have a powerful effect on market conditions. They become the new minimum market prices, because farmers do not have to sell below these rates; they may borrow from the Commodity Credit Corporation (CCC) instead and forfeit their harvest to the government. Purchasers of farm products must bid at least the per bushel loan rate to induce farmers to sell. The loan rates establish minimum market prices for all farmers, whether they participate in government programs or not. Actually, most of these non-recourse loans are made to farmers by local private banks, but the CCC will take over the loans of farmers who default and repay with their crops.

As the farm program evolved, in some cases the Commodity Credit Corporation would buy crops from farmers at a *target price,* which was the parity price or a certain fraction of it. The government would make cash payments directly to farmers rather than offer them loans, and it would assume the responsibility for storing vast amounts of farm products. This is still the practice for surplus dried milk, butter, and cheese, which the government purchases from dairy cooperatives.

If loan rates or target prices drive market prices up too high, foreign producers of cheaper agricultural products will be able to undersell American farmers in world markets, and even in American markets if there are no protectionist measures. One constant

68

criticism of government price supports is that they make American farm products uncompetitive and destroy export markets. But in the 1930s the government had given up on exports as a reliable source of income for farmers. Cotton exports, for example, fell from 14 million bales in 1929 to 3.5 million bales in 1938. Wheat exports totaled 131 million bushels (46 million hl) in 1931, but by 1934 the United States was importing more wheat than it was exporting.

Whichever method is used—direct cash payments or non-recourse loans—the difference between a low market price and the target price or loan rate is known as a *deficiency payment*. The crops for which these payments are made are known as *program crops*; they currently include wheat, barley, oats, corn, rice, soybeans, cotton, and sorghum. With either method of price support, the government undertakes either to destroy or to store large quantities of food in order to keep it off the market.

Deficiency payments are also made to wool producers. Each year the Department of Agriculture calculates the difference between the average market price received by wool producers and the ideal support price. It then makes a direct cash payment to the producers to supplement their income. But this program is unique. Wool is considered a *deficit commodity*—that is, American ranchers do not produce enough wool to satisfy consumer demand, and the balance is provided by foreign producers. The purpose of income support for other commodities is to help farmers restrict their production. But the purpose of supporting wool is to encourage domestic production against foreign competition. For this reason, deficiency payments to wool producers are also accompanied by tariffs on foreign wool and quotas on foreign-manufactured clothing. Similar tariffs and quotas protect domestic sugar producers against cheap imported sugar.

As farm programs were modified by Congress over the years, new mechanisms were introduced to support prices. A variation on the non-recourse loan is the *marketing loan.* Here farmers also receive a government loan at the established loan rate, but they are not allowed to default on the loan and hand their crops over to the government. They must sell their crops in the marketplace, but if the market price is lower than the loan rate, they need only repay whatever sum they are able to obtain from the sale. Whenever market prices are low—lower than the established loan rates—farmers get to keep the difference between their government loan and their income from their crops. This guarantees them a minimum income for a certain-size harvest. Marketing loans are now the preferred method of price support for cotton, rice, and honey.

Instead of taking out a loan, farmers may make a *purchase agreement* with the Commodity Credit Corporation. The CCC agrees to purchase the farmers' crops at some time after harvest at the current target price or loan rate. The farmers are again guaranteed an income for their crops without having to worry about low market prices. If they do not need the loan money immediately, or if they lack the storage facilities—silos, bins, corncribs, and warehouses—needed to keep the crop off the market for long periods while they wait for better prices, the purchase agreement may be preferable to a loan.

Other techniques of price manipulation include the federal *market order* and the *marketing agreement.* The market order does not depend on a support price; it is more in the nature of a mandatory production control. It is issued by the secretary of agriculture to all of the wholesale distributors of a particular farm product in a particular region, and it requires them to bring to market only a specified total quantity of that product. The surplus is not taken by the government; it is sold by the wholesalers in some other market for whatever they can get. Under a milk market order, for example, the government allows a group of regional dairy cooperatives, known as a "milk shed," to restrict the supply of fresh milk in order to keep its price high. Surplus milk is then sold at a lower price to food processors.

Marketing agreements also do not depend on price supports. They are complex agreements between producers and the government that restrict supply by carefully regulating the size, grade, quality, maturity, and other characteristics of farm products such as fruits, vegetables, and nuts. Only the highest grades of such products can be sold as fresh produce. The lower grades are sold to canners and producers of frozen foods.

Before moving on, the reader deserves a word of encouragement. If you have stayed with the narrative this far, mastering the concepts behind parity ratios, target prices, loan rates, deficiency payments, purchase agreements, and market orders, you probably have a better understanding of government agricultural policy than most of your fellow citizens. If these concepts are still hazy to you, just remember that, if farmers agree to participate in the program, the government has a variety of mechanisms at its disposal to guarantee these farmers a minimum price for their crops, if they agree to government controls over the amount of acreage that they plant. That is the basic strategy of the farm program. In theory, if the acreage planted and the resulting harvest can be reduced, scarcity will cause market prices to rise, making it unnecessary for the government to dole out money to farmers through artificial price supports. If market prices do not rise, however, all these deficiency payments and reimbursements for acreage reduction are likely to cost the government and the taxpayers a lot of money.

The farm program also created an expanded Farm Credit System, a network of banks, some federally operated—including the land banks of the Wilson administration—some privately owned, some owned by the producer cooperatives who would borrow from them. These banks made easier credit available to farmers and helped refinance debt and mortgages. Those low-income farmers unable to get loans at acceptable interest rates from these banks could turn to a new agency, the Farmers Home Administration (FHA), for loans on more generous terms.

Easy credit, the buying up of surplus farm products, deficiency payments to farmers to guarantee price levels, and incentives to take land out of production—these were the basic features of the New Deal farm program, and with some modifications they are still the tools used by the Department of Agriculture today to control surplus farm production and to provide income stability for the family farmer.

Initially, the farm program was a modest success. Surpluses were reduced. Easier credit helped many farm families avoid bankruptcy and stay on their land. Farm prices—market prices, that is—rose somewhat, but not enough to reach target prices, the mandated level of parity that would have made it unnecessary for the government to make deficiency payments to support prices. Nor did the destruction and hoarding of food by the government to raise farm prices, at a time when millions were hungry for lack of income to pay those prices, seem like a rational act. It was no less rational, however, than the Great Depression itself, in which unemployment matched unused industrial capacity and poverty existed along with the overproduction of goods.

VI

The *Flaws in the Farm Program*

Serious practical problems with the farm program became evident fairly quickly. Few people realized how many agricultural workers were tenant farmers or sharecroppers working someone else's land. In the southern states the figure was as high as 25 percent of farmworkers. The owners of the land found that they could manipulate the rules of the various soil conservation and acreage reduction programs to completely close down the operations of these tenants, throw them off their farms, and receive government payments for retiring the land from production. Throughout the South and the Midwest, many non-owner farmers were driven from the land they cultivated by the very program that was designed to keep them on the land.

A deeper flaw in the farm program was that its attack on farm surpluses was based on reducing the amount of land that was planted, not on controlling the actual amount of food that was produced. It seemed logical to assume that a reduction in the total acreage planted would lead to reduced harvests, but that did not happen. Instead, over the next two decades farm surpluses, greater than ever before, kept returning to haunt farmers and the government.

First of all, farmers, especially the richer farmers with more land to manipulate, found that they could cheat. They could include their poorer or generally unproductive land in the acreage-reduction allotment and cultivate a smaller amount of better land more intensively. They would be paid by the government for not cultivating land that was not profitable to cultivate anyway, and on their better land they would increase their yields.

There was no incentive in the farm program for the individual farmer to actually reduce production. Protected from low market prices by government price supports, farmers had every reason to grow as much as they could and then to sell their crops to the government if they could do no better elsewhere. Some could afford to reduce their acreage and also to make further investments in their remaining land so as to increase harvests. Thus, they were able to profit from the program while working against the purpose of the program.

The incentive to overproduce continues to plague farm programs down to the present day. The selective retirement of unproductive land is seen as an abuse of the program. Critics claim that large farms and corporate farms unfairly take the bulk of federal land-retirement payments for not growing on lands held just for the purpose of getting government money. Recent farm laws have tried to impose a $50,000 limit on the amount that can be paid to a single farm operation for acreage reduction, but powerful farm interests represented in Congress have ensured that there are many exceptions. Other projects of the New Deal period—land-reclamation projects designed to put people to work clearing deserts and marshes and to recover *more* land for farmers—seemed totally at odds with acreage-reduction programs.

The failure of acreage controls to reduce farm surpluses was foreordained for a more fundamental reason. The revolution in American agricultural technology was far from over. It was in fact entering a new phase in which mechanical, biological, and chemical innovations would boost harvests beyond all expectations. During the 1940s and 1950s, with the perfection of the gasoline engine, farmers began purchasing a new generation of combines—self-propelled, tractorless machines that could harvest, thresh, sort, and clean the crops, thus reducing labor at harvest time and eliminating a lot of spoilage. One machine, operated by one individual, could move through the fields propelled by its own engine, cutting the crops, threshing or removing the grain from the stalks, separating out the straw and chaff and unwanted seeds of grass and weeds, and packing the cleaned grain into convenient bins or bags.

Before the appearance of the combine, farmers were in the habit of cutting their grain several weeks before it was actually ripe so that the heads of grain— the seed kernels—would not blow away in the wind. The shocks of bundled grain were left in the fields and not threshed until ripe, and inevitably some of it rotted. The combine harvester eliminated the need for premature reaping, and the entire harvesting operation could be conducted at one time. With different mechanical adaptations, combines can be used to harvest wheat, barley, oats, rye, corn, rice, soybeans, and sorghum. Other sophisticated mechanical devices can even pick potatoes, lettuce, cucumbers, and onions. There are now machines that gently shake the branches of peach and apple trees and catch the falling fruit. By 1975, almost 75 percent of the nation's vegetable harvest was mechanically picked.

During this same period, rural electrification projects reached out into remote areas of the country, so that by 1969 more than 98 percent of the nation's farms had electricity. Here was a new power source

Due to advances in farm machinery, harvests have increased beyond expectations. This tractor is seeding grain.

for lighting, power tools, pumps, milking machines, and other farm equipment.

Antibiotics became available and were added to animal feed to protect livestock from disease. The development of techniques of artificial insemination was an enormous boon to the dairy industry because, as city dwellers are sometimes surprised to learn, cows must be pregnant to give milk. From 1930 to 1970, the number of gasoline tractors employed on farms increased from 900,000 to almost 5 million, the number of combines from 60,000 to more than 800,000, and the amount of commercial fertilizer from 8 million short tons to nearly 40 million short tons. During the same period, farm output doubled.

The revolution in farm machinery was complemented by a revolution in the genetic management of the crops themselves. It began with the introduction of hybrid corn. Farmers had been experimenting with corn ever since they inherited the plant from the Indians, selecting as seed for the next crop only kernels from the best ears, and over time corn had grown in size and nutritiousness. But farmers' corn grows in the open fields, and wind-blown pollen from other corn plants can fertilize the improved varieties, making their genetic heritage unstable. Hybrid corn was the work of scientists.

Before the turn of the century, botanists, in their search for plants that would produce higher yields, had succeeded in inbreeding pure varieties of corn. But in the early 1900s, Edward M. East of the Connecticut Agricultural Experiment Station and George H. Shull of the Cold Spring Experiment Station on Long Island demonstrated that pure inbred lines of corn produced lower yields and that this problem could be solved by hybridizing, or crossing, two inbred lines. The daughter corn plant produced higher yields and was said to possess "hybrid vigor." In 1917, Donald Jones, also of the Connecticut Agricultural Experiment Station, perfected a method of "double-cross-breeding" pure lines of corn so that the hybrid offspring retained the desired genetic traits. Hybrid corn produced yields up to 25 percent higher than those of the varieties farmers had been using.

As a young man writing for his father's farm magazine, Henry A. Wallace, the future secretary of agriculture, took an interest in the work of East, Shull, and Jones and began experimenting with hybrid corn himself. In 1926 he founded the Pioneer Hi-Bred Corn Company and began marketing his Copper Cross hybrid seed to Iowa farmers. Other hybrid seed companies were soon established, and farmers couldn't get enough of the improved seed. In 1933 less than 1 percent of the land in the Iowa cornbelt was planted with hybrid seed. By 1944, eleven years later, the figure was 88 percent. By the 1960s, more than 95 percent of all the corn harvested in the United States was grown from hybrid seed. Yields were increased, and this corn could be bred for proper stiffness of stalk and uniform height so that the new combines could reap them more efficiently.

Corn, of course, is grown principally as livestock feed, and cheaper and more plentiful feed grains meant cheaper and more plentiful cattle, chickens, and hogs and higher meat consumption for Americans, as well as increased quantities of milk, cheese, and eggs. Soon plant geneticists were initiating a veritable "green revolution" as they improved the seeds of other cereal grains. The DeKalb Seed Company introduced hybrid sorghum in 1956 and by the 1970s was working on hybrid cotton and hybrid sunflower seeds. In 1942, Henry A. Wallace's son, Henry B. Wallace, introduced hybrid chickens through the Pioneer Hi-Bred Corn Company, and hybrid hogs and cattle soon followed. In the 1950s, Dr. Norman Borlaug developed a new strain of "dwarf wheat" that produced larger heads of grain and was easier to harvest. Suddenly it seemed miraculously easy to get more food out of the ground simply by planting genetically improved seeds.

Of course, it wasn't really that easy. These new selectively bred grains did give higher yields per bushel, but large fields of plants with uniform genetic characteristics were more susceptible to disease and insect pests, so they had to be protected with larger doses of pesticides and herbicides. The extra food in the larger heads of grain required larger doses of artificial fertilizers and growth-regulating chemicals. Green revolution seeds required a revolutionary expansion of the agricultural chemical industry.

This revolution in technique transformed American agriculture. Farming became *intensive,* a carefully directed process in which farmers as business managers applied certain inputs—seed, fertilizer, machinery, gasoline, pesticide—to their land to maximize their output. Their activity became known as *industrial* farming because of its use of complex machinery, fuel, and chemicals derived from the petroleum industry. In addition to their knowledge of the soil and the weather, farmers now had to understand production planning, mechanical engineering, and cost accounting. They needed a working knowledge of commodities markets and government regulations as well.

Farmers also became more deeply indebted to the bank, because the new combines and chemicals were expensive. So too was the new hybrid seed. But in the open fields hybrid corn would soon cross-pollinate with other varieties and lose its vigor, so farmers had to return to the seed companies every year for a new supply. In this way they incurred a new cost and a new unbreakable link to the burgeoning seed industry.

American farmers still thought of themselves as hardworking individualists, but they were involved in a deepening web of dependency that tied them to banks and lending institutions, railroad and trucking industries, seed and petrochemical companies, oil refineries, manufacturers of tractors and harvesters, food processors, and government agencies. It was this new integrated farming system that led Harvard professor and former assistant secretary of agriculture John H. Davis in 1955 to coin the word *agribusiness* to describe American farming in the modern era.

The evolving agribusiness system was extraordinary. Some Marxist critics predicted that, as capitalism developed, large corporate farming operations would gobble up most small farms, and farmers would become landless agricultural workers in a vast network of large factorylike commercial farms. It was a grim vision, and certainly large corporate farms have appeared and become a major force in agricultural production. It is also true that many of the larger family farms are run more and more like factories.

But the agribusiness system evolved in a different way than the Marxists expected. In a process economists call *vertical integration*, the system has retained at its core a large population of independent family-owned and -operated farms. These farms form a base of producer-suppliers of agricultural raw materials in a hierarchy of manufacturers and middlemen, and because of their numbers, their productivity, and their competitiveness, farmers within this system have little power to influence prices or control their economic circumstances.

We have already seen how, through increasing mechanization and improvements in biotechnology and biochemistry, farmers became dependent on the suppliers of industrial products. Modern farming would be impossible without an advanced industrial economy. Furthermore, with the continuing merchandizing revolution, farmers became a smaller and smaller part of the overall food production system, increasingly alienated from the consumer, their economic contribution masked behind the activities of food processing companies and supermarket chains. Today only about 25 percent or less of the retail price of food goes to the farmer. The remaining 75 percent is divided up among millers, merchants, transporters, food processors, and retailers. This includes about 3 to 4 percent for advertising and promotion, and 9 percent for packaging. A new labor contract at a major breakfast cereal company is now likely to have a greater impact on consumer prices than what the farmer receives for a bushel of corn or wheat. In 1982, for example, the national food bill was $298 billion, but only $84 billion was paid to farmers.

Supermarkets also revolutionized American buying habits and changed the way farmers did business. The Safeway Company, for example, was founded in California in 1926 and by the mid-1970s had grown into a chain of 2,500 supermarkets worldwide with 135,000 employees and profits of more than $2 billion. To supply these retail stores, Safeway acquired and operated its own bakeries, meatpacking and poultry plants, fruit and vegetable canneries, frozen food factories, coffee-roasting and egg-candling operations, and plants making jellies, candies, soups, cereals, and soft drinks.

Such a large food conglomerate requires a lot of agricultural products and is in a position to bargain effectively for them. Farmers in various regions of the country developed steady relationships with these large processing-retailing organizations and began to produce for them under contract for a guaranteed price at harvest time. By the 1970s most poultry, most sugarcane, and about two-thirds of the vegetables not sold as fresh produce were grown under contract and sold to canners, freezers, refiners, and other food processors. Most fresh milk and citrus fruits were sold under contract to producer cooperatives. The guaranteed prices were a protection against fluctuations in market prices, but they created a new dependency on the middlemen of the food production system. Now even decisions about which crops to grow may be made not by farmers but by processors and retailers through the contract system.

Only 3 percent of American farms are corporate farms, and most of these are family-owned operations that have simply grown too large to be run only by family labor. There is considerable concentration of economic power in these farms, however. Large farms, those with sales of $100,000 or more, constitute only 6 percent of the total number of farms, but they account for more than 50 percent of the nation's farm output. The number of such large commercial farms began to grow rapidly in the 1960s and 1970s, raising concerns about corporate control of agriculture, the environmental effects of intensive farming, the confinement of animals in "factory farms," and the loss of quality and genetic diversity in our food supply. These are serious issues that we will explore on pages 113–114.

The agribusiness system has not converted most family farms into corporate farms. There is extensive

A 1990 tractor

corporate control of American agriculture through ownership of the manufacturers of farm supplies and equipment and through ownership of the grain trading companies, food processors, and food retailers who buy what farmers produce. It was unnecessary for large corporations involved in food processing to

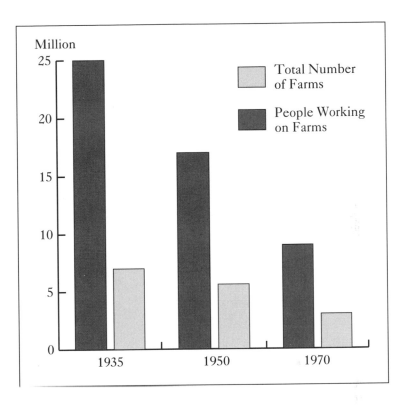

Decline in Numbers of Farms and Farm-jobs

actually take over and operate the farms. The farms—with their low profit margins, endless debt problems, and dependence on non-economic factors (such as soil and weather)—did not appear to be attractive investments.

The breakthroughs in machine technology, agricultural chemistry, and plant genetics of the 1940s and 1950s enabled farmers to vastly increase the size of their harvests even as they participated in government programs to reduce the number of acres they planted. By the early 1960s, one farmer could grow enough food to feed twenty-eight people, and, by the early 1970s, almost fifty people. It proved impossible to take enough land out of agricultural production to compensate for the increased productivity of farmers. Consequently, surpluses continued to wreak havoc with farm prices and farm incomes.

While the prices for wheat and corn fluctuated because millions of farmers were competing in an uncertain marketplace, the prices of tractors and combines and chemicals were relatively fixed because farmers had to buy from a small number of large manufacturing firms. The cost-price squeeze grew tighter as farmers, even with government-guaranteed prices, had to finance the purchase of new machines, fuel, petrochemicals, seed, and new silos and farm buildings. The amount of capital investment a farmer had to make to operate a farm had grown astronomically, with the result that it became harder for young farmers to get into the business or to take over from their parents.

As a result, in spite of the stated purpose of government programs, people began leaving farming in great numbers in the mid-1930s. In 1935 approximately 25 million Americans worked on just under 7 million farms, but the total number of farms began to decline at that point by about 1 million every decade and the number of farmers by about 1 million every year. By 1950 approximately 17 million Americans worked on just 5.6 million farms, and by 1970 a little more than 9 million Americans worked on fewer than 3 million farms.

The land didn't just disappear, of course. It was purchased and absorbed into the surviving farms, which grew bigger. In 1935 the size of the average American farm was 160 acres (almost 65 ha). By 1950 it was about 200 acres (81 ha), and by 1970 almost

375 acres (almost 152 ha). But there were fewer farmers, and those that remained were still struggling with mountains of surplus grain. In fact, farm incomes were not significantly improved by government programs, and farmers did not experience another period of prosperity until World War II, when they again increased production and sold their surpluses to feed war-ravaged nations. Once again, however, their situation worsened when the war ended and they could not reduce the size of their harvests.

VII

Prosperity and Crisis

The problem that American farmers face today is a continuation of the problem they have faced for more than a century, but it is also rooted in a specific series of events that occurred in the previous two decades—a period of unprecedented prosperity during the 1970s, which created the conditions for a terrible farm debt crisis in the 1980s.

After World War II, American farm exports declined again as the Europeans were able to replant their fields in peace and farmers in Australia, New Zealand, Canada, and Argentina put part of their harvests up for sale in international markets. American grain, critics say, had become overpriced by government price supports. During the 1950s and 1960s farmers struggled on, but the number of farms declined from 5.6 million in 1950 to 3.9 million in 1960, and to 2.9 million by 1970. The remaining farms grew larger, more commercialized, and more specialized as they became increasingly integrated into the agribusiness system. All the while, many farmers were kept afloat by government loans and crop purchases, and the government began to accumulate large surpluses of farm products that were becoming expensive to store. Still, throughout the 1950s and 1960s, federal deficiency payments were never more than 10 percent of total farm income, and the cost of price supports to the taxpayer was $3 billion to $4 billion annually, a modest amount by later standards. This muted criticism of the program, and farm interests were still powerful enough to throw their weight for or against other legislation, so they were courted or appeased by other political groups in Congress.

The growing surpluses, however, did trouble politicians. In 1954 Congress passed Public Law 480, the Farm Surplus Disposal Act. Called the "Food for Peace" program in the 1960s by President John F. Kennedy, P.L. 480 was intended as an export-enhancement program that would dispose of surplus food through giveaways for famine relief and long-term low-interest loans to foreign countries to purchase American farm products. In the 1960s the Food for Peace program was able to dispose of about 16 million tons of food a year. In 1964 Congress passed the Food Stamp Act to "raise the level of nutrition among low-income households" by issuing subsidized coupons for the purchase of food. The Food and Nutrition Service of the Department of Agriculture also administers a National School Lunch Program, a Child Care Food Program, and a Special Milk Program, all of which provide needed assistance to the poor while attempting to reduce government food stocks.

These programs hardly made a dent in the huge surpluses farmers were producing, however. Even with significant poverty in the United States, there were natural limits to how much Americans could increase their food consumption. The nation's population would have to instantly double to create enough domestic demand for food to eliminate farm surpluses. And yet during the 1970s an unusual series of events accomplished just that—the virtual elimination of farm surpluses—and gave farmers their highest income in decades.

When Richard Nixon assumed the presidency in 1970, he faced a serious balance-of-payments problem. Because of declining exports and rising imports, and because of expenses related to the Vietnam War, dollars were flowing out of the country and accumulating in foreign accounts. Because the United States was on the gold standard, these foreign holders of American dollars could redeem them in gold, depleting stocks in the U.S. Treasury. On August 15, 1971, Nixon effectively took the United States off the gold standard by announcing that the government would no longer freely convert foreign-held dollars into gold. This had the effect of devaluing the dollar, making it less valuable in relation to other currencies, and consequently making American goods less expensive in foreign markets. This stimulated the sale of American farm products abroad, and farm prices began to rise. In the early 1970s wheat went from $1.54 a bushel to $2.26 a bushel, and corn from $1.04 a bushel to $1.35 a bushel.

Devastating famines in Africa and Asia during the early 1970s also helped to deplete world stocks of grain. A United Nations World Food Conference was convened in Rome in 1974 to discuss the famines in India, Bangladesh, and sub-Saharan Africa. Grim reports were presented documenting widespread starvation caused by overpopulation and grain shortages brought about by bad weather. The famine relief programs that emerged would be supported in large part by American farm surpluses. At the same time, in countries that were not suffering famine, there was a general trend to upgrade diets with more meat. Since a steer must eat about 16 pounds (7 kg) of feed grain to produce 1 pound (about 0.5 kg) of beef, higher meat consumption meant huge increases in grain consumption. And off the coast of Peru in the early

90

1970s, the warm waters of the Pacific current known as El Niño swept into the anchovy fishing grounds and wiped them out. Anchovy meal was used as a protein supplement in feed for cattle and poultry, and Peruvian fisheries had supplied 80 percent of the worldwide demand. This further increased demand for American feed grains, especially the protein-rich soybean, which went from $3.00 a bushel to more than $12.00 a bushel in 1973.

Nixon, like many recent presidents, had little interest in agriculture himself, but he appointed as his secretary of agriculture Earl Butz, a conservative who passionately disliked farm programs and the whole idea of the government paying farmers anything and attempting to manage production. He openly criticized payments to farmers as a form of welfare. Butz wanted to get the government out of agriculture completely and return farmers to dependence on the marketplace. He would do this by encouraging the new surge in exports to eliminate farm surpluses and by changing the farm program to make it ineffective.

The basic farm program is modified and reauthorized by Congress about every five years. The farm bill that Butz crafted and Congress passed in 1973, the Agriculture and Consumer Protection Act, was unique in that it set target prices very low and limited payments to individual farmers to a maximum of $20,000. The target price for wheat, for example, was set at $2.05 a bushel. At the time the new law went into effect, the market price for a bushel of wheat was $4.59, and by August 1973 it had risen to $5.00 a bushel. No farmer in his right mind would forfeit his crop to the government for a loan at a rate of $2.05 a bushel when he could earn more than twice as much by selling in the marketplace. And with market prices so much higher than target prices, there was no need for deficiency payments to farmers. Price support mechanisms became inoperative. Whereas, during the late 1960s, government payments to farmers had averaged about 20 percent of their total income, during the 1970s farmers were receiving on average no more than 5 percent of their income from the government.

The 1973 farm bill also ended the acreage reduction program, eliminating all restrictions on the amount of land that farmers could plant. Responding to increasing foreign demand, American farmers took 38 million acres (15 million ha) of land they had idled to receive parity payments and put them into production. Secretary Butz, government experts, and private economists, envisioning a new role for American farmers in feeding the world, urged them to plant from "fencerow to fencerow," confident that all these favorable conditions would last. William Mueller writes in the winter 1987 issue of the *American Scholar* that farmers "purchased land because bankers told them it was wise to leverage themselves into a higher debt structure. They bought new equipment because agricultural experts told them that to buy this year was the only shelter against next year's inflation and that expansion was the way of the future." The demand for new fields caused the price of land to rise, and farmers increased their indebtedness to finance their expanded operations. But farmers weren't worried because they were receiving record-high prices and incomes. In 1972 the nation's agricultural exports were worth $6.7 billion. By 1974 they were worth $20.4 billion and had even created a trade surplus and a favorable balance-of-payments situation for the United States. From 1970 to 1980 the nation's wheat harvest increased from 1.4 billion bushels (493 million hl) to 2.4 billion bushels (846 million hl); the corn harvest grew from 4.1 billion bushels (1.4 billion hl) in 1972 to 6.6 billion bushels, (2.3 billion hl) in 1982. What all this increased output would do to farm surpluses did not trouble Secretary Butz at all, for there were no more farm surpluses, in part because of the general increase in farm exports, but largely because of an incredible stroke of luck for Butz and for American farmers—the great Russian grain deal.

In 1972 there were serious crop failures in the Soviet Union. Soviet citzens were never in danger of starving in the streets, but the grain shortfall made it impossible for the Soviets to fulfill a commitment in their current five-year plan to raise the level of their citizens' consumption of meat. They had already purchased prime cattle and poultry from the United States and Canada to be used as breeding stock in expanding their livestock industry. Now they lacked the grain to feed their animals. Rather than renege on their commitment to improve diets, the Soviets chose to purchase massive quantities of foreign grain in world markets. In spite of political frictions, the United States authorized American grain merchants to sell to the Soviets. In the summer of 1972 the Soviet Union purchased 29 million metric tons of grain in international markets, including 19 million metric tons from the United States—12 million metric tons of wheat, 6 million of corn, and 1 million of soybeans. (A metric ton equals 1,000 kilograms. A kilogram—or a kilo, as it is known to international air travelers—is approximately 2.2 pounds. So a metric ton weighs about 2,200 pounds, being a little heavier than the English ton of 2,000 pounds.) Another Soviet purchase of 14.6 million metric tons of American grain occurred in 1975. So anxious was Butz to consummate the sale that the Department of Agriculture even gave the Russians $750 million in low-interest loans to help pay for the grain. And with good reason—in a very short time, farm surpluses disappeared completely. The cost of storing the surplus alone had been averaging almost $650 million a year. The price of space on the world's fleet of merchant ships skyrocketed as freighters were reserved to transport 29 million tons of food to the Soviet Union. The Soviets used the high-quality American grain to feed their people and were able to divert a portion of their own remaining poorer-quality grain for livestock feed.

Butz's success was complete. Suddenly, for the first time in four decades, farmers were prospering in the marketplace, the surpluses were gone, and expensive government price supports and acreage controls had become unnecessary. Exports were the key. Depression-era economists had been wrong, it was now believed, to advocate restricting farm production, abandoning world markets and suggesting that farmers produce only to satisfy the domestic market. American farmers had to compete beyond their borders in free markets without government interference, Butz believed, and the export boom proved that they could do it.

The prosperity of farmers was not appreciated by everybody, however. American consumers got a taste of what it was like to shop in a marketplace where there were no huge reserves of food to depress prices. In January 1973 food prices rose by 20 percent in one month. In 1974 the price of sugar rose from 11 cents a pound to 60 cents a pound. American consumers, who had paid $141 billion for food in 1971, were paying $226 billion for food by 1976. Consumers reacted angrily by boycotting meat producers, whose high prices reflected the increasing cost of feed grains, and in the public eye the great Russian grain deal came to be known as the great Russian grain robbery. Paying farmers not to grow food had always seemed slightly irrational. But now Americans, through their food bills, were paying the full cost of a free market in which they were competing with foreign consumers for their own farm products, and they did not like it.

In the midst of a period of increased production *and* increased farm income, no one was willing to look too closely at a new set of problems that were developing. All this expanded production was increasing farmers' costs and driving up their indebtedness. By 1976 farmland was selling for $2,000 an acre, and a farmer needed to work at least 3,000 acres (over 1,200 ha) of wheat or 1,000 acres (about 405 ha) of corn in order to afford a modern tractor, which might cost as much as $50,000. Then, in October 1973, the Organization of Petroleum Exporting Countries, OPEC, imposed an embargo on oil exports that lasted until March 1974. In modern farming, petroleum is a farmer's single largest input. Now there was a shortage of gasoline and the petrochemicals used in artificial fertilizers. The price of fuel rose by 400 percent and the price of fertilizers by 1,000 percent. Though the price of wheat was running well over $4.00 a bushel, a wheat farmer now needed a price of $3.50 a bushel to cover his costs. Everything would be all right as long as there was a strong foreign demand for American grain and farm prices stayed high enough for farmers to cover their costs and loan repayments. Food exports had become America's largest source of foreign exchange, and farm prosperity now depended on exporting 25 percent of the corn crop, 50 percent of the soybean crop, and more than 60 percent of the wheat crop.

But the export market was about to collapse, partly because the government lost the courage of its

convictions. In June 1973, fearful of domestic shortages, President Nixon prohibited the export of soybeans. In 1974 and 1975, for similar reasons,
President Gerald Ford put additional restrictions on
grain sales to foreign countries. Then in January
1980, in the biggest blow yet to American farmers,
President Jimmy Carter embargoed the sale of grain
to the Soviet Union in response to the Soviet invasion
of Afghanistan. As a result of the earlier restrictions,
farm surpluses had started to build up again as early
as 1975, but now they began mounting rapidly as
American farm exports declined from a value of $44
billion in 1981 to $26 billion by 1986.

As farm income declined, price supports kicked
back into effect. Not only were farmers again being
supported by the government, but the guaranteed
price levels provided grain producers in Canada,
Argentina, Brazil, and Australia with a further incentive to sell their cheaper grain in world markets and
further undercut American exports. Because of all the
embargoes and restrictions, grain-importing countries began to turn to these other producers, regarding
American suppliers as unreliable. Generally, during
the 1980s, grain production in foreign countries was
increasing at the rate of 29 million tons a year, reducing the need to import from the United States. The
technological revolution in agriculture had had an
impact on farmers in other countries, who were now
able to produce grain more cheaply than American
farmers, with their artificial price supports. America's
share of the world market for agricultural products
fell from a high of 19.3 percent in 1981 to 14.8 percent in 1987. During the same period, the U.S. share
of the world market for feed grains alone fell from 72
percent to 38 percent. Farmers discovered that the
export market, though attractive, was unreliable and

could fluctuate wildly, depending on all kinds of political and economic events beyond their control. The government and economic experts had urged farmers to increase production, but now they had left farmers hanging in the wind.

In 1983 the administration of President Ronald Reagan made an innovative attempt to reduce farm surpluses with the Payment-in-Kind program. If farmers would agree to take a good portion—up to 30 percent—of their land out of production, the Department of Agriculture would issue those farmers PIK certificates redeemable in government surplus grain, which the farmers were then free to sell in the marketplace in place of the crop they would have grown themselves. The farmers would receive an adequate income, and surpluses would be rapidly reduced. As conceived in 1983, however, the program did not work well. Farmers did leave 77 million acres (31 million ha) of cropland idle in exchange for $10 billion worth of government surplus food, but they were required to actually take possession of the grain or dairy products when they exchanged their PIK certificates, and this proved to be a transport and storage nightmare all across the country.

The Payment-in-Kind program was revised in 1986. The PIK certificates were no longer denominated in bushels of wheat or corn or rice but in dollars, and farmers were no longer required to hand them back to the government and haul away surplus grain. They could trade or sell or auction off their PIK certificates to other parties—grain merchants, food processors, commodities speculators, other farmers—anyone with a need to obtain the raw materials of food. The PIK certificates became a new kind of currency, backed by stocks of grain rather than gold, and many farmers began to trade or hoard the certificates as they acquired a market price higher than their face value. Farmers who are about to bring in their harvests desperately need storage space, which was in very short supply because of government surpluses. With a PIK certificate, those farmers had a claim on the cleared storage space if they took a quantity of government grain for sale. So the rising price of the PIK certificates reflected the demand for storage facilities as well as the price of the grain.

There was some irony in the fact that this new variation on the government's program of farm subsidies was crafted by the conservatives of the Reagan administration. It worked in ways that nobody expected, and more than anything else it deepened the commitment of the government to manage agriculture and made farmers even more dependent on government programs. By the late 1980s about 30 percent of government subsidies to farmers were in the form of PIK certificates. The rest were in the form of the conventional farm support mechanisms that were still in effect—cash payments, loans, and deficiency payments. Though the program provided income for farmers who stopped or decreased production, it devastated the underlying network of farm suppliers—the manufacturers of tractors, combines, and fertilizers, and the suppliers of seed. Agribusiness losses have been estimated at $4 billion in lost sales and a loss of 250,000 jobs, including seasonal field hands. In 1984 the Small Business Administration paid out $24.3 million in loans to fertilizer companies to save them from the reduced demand for their products. Between 1979 and 1984 almost 25 percent of farm dealerships went out of business.

The Payment-in-Kind program had another unintended and calamitous effect. It had not actually eliminated the surplus; it had simply put it into the hands of farmers, who now had to sell it to survive. Large amounts of farm products began to flood the marketplace, depressing prices. Price supports had made American grain too expensive for foreign buyers, and exports had collapsed. Third World nations were experiencing a debt crisis, having borrowed heavily from the industrialized nations during the 1970s, and they were now having difficulty paying for American grain. The technological revolution had enabled farmers to grow still more on even less acreage, so that in spite of all the farmland idled by the PIK program, the 1985 corn crop, for example, was a record 8.8 billion bushels (3.1 billion hl). And now this government dumping of the farm surplus into the marketplace only made things worse. Corn farmers, who were used to getting $4.00 a bushel in the early 1970s, were receiving no more than $1.50 a bushel by the mid-1980s. As farm prices fell, the size of government deficiency payments rose. The target price for corn in the mid-1980s was more than $2.00 a bushel, so the government paid farmers about 50 cents for every bushel they sold.

Meanwhile, a new agricultural crisis was developing. Desperate for protection against low market prices, farmers began to participate in the government farm program in record numbers. David Rapp, in his book *How the U.S. Got into Agriculture and Why It Can't Get Out,* describes how in 1982 only 20 percent of Indiana corn farmers were enrolled in the farm program: "In Indiana, taking money from the federal government was a sign of poor farm management or, worse, socialistic political tendencies." But by 1987, attitudes had changed and more than 50 percent of Indiana corn farmers were receiving price supports. Nationally, the percentage of wheat farmers participating in government programs went from 60 percent in 1981 to 84 percent in 1986. With market prices falling, many banks and agricultural lending institutions refused to make loans unless farmers were protected by government subsidies. All these new farmers receiving more loans and larger and larger deficiency payments began to have its effect. The cost of the farm program went up to $13 billion in 1985, $23 billion in 1986, and a record $26 billion in 1987. The farm program grew into the government's third largest benefit program after Social Security and Medicare.

Between 1981 and 1987 average farm income fell by 55 percent because of recurring surpluses and low market prices. As farm income fell, many farmers began to have trouble repaying the loans they had used for expansion during the 1970s. If farmers have to make loan payments, they may be forced to sell their crops at an inopportune time for a low market price, which will either further reduce their income or increase the size of their deficiency payments. Total farm debt had increased from $45 billion in 1975 to $186 billion in 1987. By the 1980s, there were fewer than 5 million working farmers in the United States, less than 2 percent of the population, fewer farmers than there were unemployed workers. About a third, or more than 200,000, of the nation's 600,000 middle-sized, commercial-scale family farmers were in serious debt trouble.

Viewed against the general exodus of people from farming that had been going on since the 1930s, the actual number of farm bankruptcies during the 1980s was not great. James Bovard, in his book *The Farm Fiasco,* reports that fewer than 50,000 farmers went bankrupt between 1981 and 1987. By contrast, more than 200,000 farmers went bankrupt in 1951, and more than 130,000 in 1961. During the farm crisis of the 1980s, farmers were not being driven from the land in large numbers, but their debt problems were real. The actual number of foreclosures and dispossessions was small because the debt had been transferred to the taxpayers through the farm program. It was the policy of the banks of the Farm Credit System and the Farmers Home Administration not to foreclose on debt-burdened farmers but to refinance them—that is, to make new loans whenever farmers were unable to pay the old ones. As a result, the Farm Credit System began to report losses in 1985. In 1986, Congress had to appropriate an additional $4 billion to rescue the Farm Credit System from bankruptcy. This, of course, was in addition to the cost of the price support program. From 1981 to 1987 the average annual government payment to each farmer went from $794 to $7,727, from 6 to 30 percent of total farm income, creating that enormous $26 billion government bill for farm subsidies. This prompted Steve Broder to write in *The Progressive* magazine in 1987 that "Without Government assistance, farming today is a nonprofit activity." Most of the more than 200,000 family farmers who were in financial trouble were kept in business by government subsidies, but without those subsidies their farm operations were insolvent, and it was difficult for such farmers to avoid the feeling that they had failed.

The total number of dispossessions was comparatively small, but when they did occur, they were grim affairs, often covered by the news media, in which groups of farmers were forced to watch their neighbors' possessions being auctioned off for a pittance. Families who had lived on the land for three, four, or more generations had to sell their homes and move on. Even for successful farmers and those protected by price supports, such a sight was a sobering reminder of how fragile their way of life had become. The idea of family farm ownership itself seemed threatened, since the heavily mortgaged land was the very thing that was oppressing farmers. In a few hard-hit areas, the whole character of rural life was changing. Though the land of bankrupt farms is soon bought up and planted by surrounding farmers enlarging their operations, and though production never falters, many of the small businesses in rural areas depend on the total number of customers rather than the total demand for farm supplies. As the number of farm families in a region declines, groceries and gas stations close, schools and health services are consolidated, and taxes rise as local governments struggle with failing regional economies. Staff writers for the Domestic Policy Association wrote in 1986, "A community consisting of twenty large farms is different from one consisting of two hundred smaller ones. Not only are fewer combines and silos purchased, there are also fewer homes, schools, and community groups. When farm operations are owned by large firms or land management companies, neither shareholders nor upper-level managers live in the region, and concern for the community diminishes." Among farmers, there were rises in the rates of suicide, divorce, and alcohol and drug abuse, and in some areas there was even a rise in participation in right-wing hate groups and paramilitary organizations.

Farmers were frustrated and angry—angry at a marketplace they couldn't predict or control, angry at their dependence on the government and its shifting farm policies and bad advice, angry at those who told them they were bad managers if they failed, and angry at urban political interests who were beginning to complain about the cost of the farm program. As early as 1978, members of one of the most militant farm organizations, the American Agricultural Movement, began to stage "tractorcades" in the streets of Washington and other cities, demanding more aid for farmers. In 1985 Hollywood began to portray the plight of farmers in films such as *Country, Places in the Heart,* and *The River.* Their stars—including Jane Fonda, Jessica Lange, and Sissy Spacek—appeared before an agriculture subcommittee of Congress to testify about the farm problem. In September 1985 recording artists Willie Nelson, Neil Young, and John Contee began to arrange a series of "Farm Aid" concerts to raise money for farmers who faced foreclosure.

Conditions improved somewhat for American farmers in the late 1980s. Foreign demand for American grain began to increase again, and in 1987 farm exports surged to almost $28 billion. From 1987 to 1990 the price of wheat rose from $2.42 a bushel to $3.72 a bushel, corn from $1.50 to $2.54, and soybeans from $4.78 to $7.42. Farmers were able to pay off some of their debts. The value of outstanding farm loans held by the Farm Credit System dropped from a high of $82 billion in 1983 to $51 billion in 1991. Government payments as a percentage of total farm income dropped from a high of 30 percent in 1987 to 19 percent in 1991. That 19 percent, however, meant that one-fifth of an average farmer's income still came from the taxpayers, and farmers knew they were still deeply dependent on both the federal government and the export market for survival. Their prosperity was, and is, dependent on many factors outside their control, and their economic future remains uncertain.

VIII

The *Future of the Farm Program*

The uncertainty of the future of the family
farmer is compounded by another legacy of the debt
crisis of the 1980s. The costs of the farm program during those years became an explosive political issue,
and today a fierce debate rages over whether or not
the farm program shouldn't simply be discontinued.
Critics argue that after more than sixty years of federal subsidies to farmers and the idling of millions of
acres of farmland, at great expense to the taxpayers,
the farm program has failed to solve the problem of
overproduction, failed to eliminate the farm surpluses, and failed, as a result, to secure decent market
prices for farmers. What Henry A. Wallace thought
would be a "temporary" method of dealing with an
emergency" has become a permanent and costly entitlement program that doesn't work. Every effort to
reduce the amount of acreage planted has been coun-
tered by the continuing revolution in agricultural
technology and the ingenuity of farmers in increasing
yields on their best land. The price support mechanisms themselves encourage overproduction because
the government becomes the guaranteed buyer of
whatever the farmer grows.

The dairy program, critics say, illustrates the
irrationality of government policy. In 1993 the Food
and Drug Administration finally approved the use of a
new bovine growth hormone that can be injected into
cows to increase milk production by 30 to 40 percent

per cow. Protests against the use of the hormone focused on the issue of its long-term effects on the health of milk drinkers, but there was little discussion of its effect on farmers. The United States does not need more milk. Milk production increased nationwide from 8,000 pounds (3,600 kg) per cow per year in 1965 to more than 12,000 pounds (5,400 kg) per cow per year in 1985. In recent years the Department of Agriculture has had to purchase and store 4 to 5 billion pounds (1.8–2.3 billion kg) of surplus milk annually. So troubling were milk surpluses that in 1986 the government initiated a new Dairy Termination Program, in which the USDA would buy entire herds of cows from milk producers if they would agree to stay out of the dairy business for five years. More than 1 million of the nation's 11 million dairy cows were either slaughtered or exported to other countries, and 144 of the nation's commercial milk producers received $1 million each to close down operations. Nevertheless, milk surpluses continued to increase because those farmers who did not participate in the termination program were able to raise their output.

Under such circumstances, why would dairy farmers want to produce more milk? Precisely because, at the same time that it was pushing some milk producers out of business, the government was paying other producers $22.50 a hundredweight (100 pounds, or 45 kg), more than twice the wholesale market price, to purchase their surplus milk. Now, with the bovine growth hormone and other innovations in biotechnology, milk production will continue to increase. This will not lower prices to consumers because the quantity of milk released to the marketplace is rigidly controlled by regional dairy cooperatives with the sanction of the Department of

The US Ayrshire Cow

Outstanding US Ayrshire genetics available today!

An efficient, adept grazer

Steadily increasing
production levels

One of the lowest
somatic cell producers of
all American dairy breeds

An animal resistant to heat stress

An enjoyable breed to work with

A hardy dairy animal
with superior feet and legs

No known undesirable
genetic recessives

Profitable producers for
dairymen around the world

Ayrshire Breeders Association
PO Box 1608
Brattleboro, VT 05302-1608
Tel 802-254-7460
Fax 802-254-7460

An advertisement for the Ayrshire cow boasts of its
"genetics" and its "steadily increasing production levels."

Agriculture. But this new biotechnology is expensive and can be most efficiently applied by the larger dairy operations, which also benefit the most from government payments because they have the largest surpluses to dispose of. The smaller and harder-pressed milk producers will take advantage of the whole-herd buyout programs and shut down. Because of the way the dairy program works, according to William Mueller, writing in *The American Scholar* in 1987, the effect of the bovine growth hormone "will be to convince small family farmers to get out of the dairy business while huge corporate dairy farms thrive— precisely the opposite effect that scientists envisioned when they began work on this bacteria years ago." James Bovard in *The Farm Fiasco* reports that since 1952 the number of commercial dairy farmers in the United States has fallen from 600,000 to 130,000, decreasing by about 4,800 farmers a year since 1970, and that "new revolutions in dairy production will soon mean that 5,000 large dairy operations in California could provide all the milk the United States needs."

Indeed, the critics say, the whole idea of supporting prices above market levels is irrational and goes against the natural evolution of a capitalist economy. George Easterbrook, writing in the July 1985 issue of *Atlantic Monthly*, makes the point that "A successful economy is supposed to drive down the prices of goods, especially manufactured goods—and the advent of fertilizers, pesticides, self-propelled combines, and large tractors has made agriculture one of the least labor-intensive of industries. . . . Farm groups say that there is something wrong with the fact that wheat costs less in real terms today than it did in 1870. There would be something wrong if it *didn't* cost less." As agriculture becomes more productive, it provides a cheap and abundant food supply for the growing number of non-farmworkers who make industrial growth possible. Holding prices above market levels, the critics say, is holding up progress. Price supports turn back the clock to a time when agricultural technology was less developed and farm productivity was lower because more human labor was required in farming. Food *was* more expensive in real terms, and we should not want to return to that time. Nor would farmers wish to return to the days of back-breaking labor before machines. The farm program fails to recognize that technological change is irreversible and that food *should* become cheaper.

Price supports don't even benefit the farmers who need them most. Staff writers for the Domestic Policy Association wrote in 1986 that "Subsidies are based on production, a simple dollars per bushel formula. The more you produce, the more you get. While a wheat farmer with 250 acres [100 ha] might get a support loan of $26,000, a farmer with 2,500 acres [1,000 ha] would get about ten times as much. . . . Almost 30 percent of all farm subsidies go to the largest 1 percent of all producers. Meanwhile, the 80 percent of all farmers with sales of less than $100,000 a year—the farms experiencing the greatest economic stress—receive less than a third of government payments."

Nor has the farm program been very successful at keeping struggling farmers on the land. Since 1935 the number of farms has dropped from 6.6 million to 2.2 million, and the farm population has dropped from 32 million to less than 5 million. But this should not be lamented, the critics say, for the declining farm population is a natural result of increasing farm productivity and the transition from an agrarian to an industrial economy. The labor of so many farmers is no longer needed in American agriculture, and millions of people whose parents and grandparents were farmers have found work and new lives in the cities. These economic dislocations cause many problems, but they can't be stopped. The whole idea of a government program to keep unnecessary and unprofitable farms in business was a mistake from the very beginning. Should manufacturers of television sets or refrigerators be protected by government subsidies if they continue to produce more models than people will buy? If, because of excess supply or obsolete technology or bad design, a certain model automobile should become difficult to sell and its price must be lowered, should the government give the manufacturer a deficiency payment for every car sold? Or should the government promise to buy the cars at a price far above their market value if the manufacturer can't sell them, and then rent space in junkyards to store them? When the car replaced the horse, was the government obligated to make cash payments to failing blacksmiths and wagonmakers? If someone were to discover a cure for tooth decay, would the government be obligated to support bankrupt dentists? If farming is a business, it must operate as a business, and there should be no welfare for those farmers who can't manage their farms efficiently and competitively, or who can't face the consequences of the revolution in agricultural technology.

Loans and price supports and cash payments haven't arrested the decline of the farm population, but they have kept in business hundreds of thousands of essentially bankrupt farms, at great expense at a time of large federal deficits and voter anger over high taxes. Most of these debt-burdened farmers grow more food than anyone can eat. Without government subsidies, these farmers would soon go out of business, either helping to reduce production, or transferring their land to larger, more efficiently managed farms. From the rational perspective of economics, the critics say, there really is no farm problem other than that created by the farm program, which is holding up a natural adjustment in our economy. Given the high productivity of American agriculture, the only real farm problem is that there are still too many farmers.

There is a powerful if cruel logic to this argument, which is essentially the argument of the free-market economist. If an economy keeps too many people producing more of something than consumers want, it is using human resources inefficiently, and all producers are prevented from earning a fair return for their efforts. Wouldn't it be better to eliminate price supports and to expose American farmers to the competition of the marketplace? Wouldn't it be better to allow inefficient farms to go out of business so that the remaining farmers can adjust production to the level of consumer demand and obtain fair prices through the free market?

Even most supporters of the farm program recognize that there will be fewer farmers in the future as many give up the struggle against an unpredictable income. Older farmers will retire, and young people will be discouraged from starting new farms because of the high capital investment an efficient modern farm requires. But to suddenly and dramatically end farm subsidies and to abandon farmers to their fate in the marketplace, supporters of the farm program warn, might create a new set of problems more serious than surpluses and low farm income.

First of all, driving hundreds of thousands of farmers off the land might be justifiable at a time when the economy is growing and creating new jobs elsewhere, but during a recession or a period of slow growth these bankrupt farmers either join the ranks of the unemployed or enter premature retirement. Many hidden social costs are connected with this thinning-out of the farm population. Numerous small farm-related businesses will fail, small towns will become what University of Iowa professor Michael Jacobsen has called "rural ghettos," and the values and way of life of the family farmer—so important to the evolution of American democracy—may pass out of existence.

Second, where is the guarantee that production will adjust itself simply because there are fewer farmers? The history of American farming does not support this idea. Long before there were price supports or farm programs, farmers were growing greater and greater quantities of food even as millions of people left the land. The pressure to produce more food predates price supports and is caused by the highly competitive nature of farming. To get to the point where farmers can control production and gain enough power over the marketplace to demand higher prices, we would have to have very few farmers indeed.

So if the free market rules, where will the decline in the number of farms stop, and what kind of farms and farming systems will remain? Though today 97 percent of American farms are still family-owned and only 3 percent are large corporate farms, the elimination of farm subsidies will cause many bankruptcies and accelerate the trend toward concentration of land ownership in fewer and fewer hands. Most successful family-owned farms have already become sizable commercial enterprises with an average investment in land and equipment of close to $1 million. Another farm crisis, another cycle of selling out and buying up, will transform many of these operations into super-farms, family-owned or not.

The economists Heather Ball and Leland Beatty writing in *The Nation* in 1984, evaluating the effects of proposed cuts to target prices in the then pending 1985 farm bill, suggested that the United States might lose more than 1 million farms by the year 2000 and that "what will be left is about 50,000 large farms producing 75 percent of all food, and the rest will be small farms used for residences, alternative products, truck farms, and of course tax shelters. . . . Evidence suggests that if control of food is concentrated into 50,000 units around the country, food prices will soar." Of course, critics of farm subsidies would say, that's just the point. Let consumers save billions of dollars in taxes by the elimination of price supports and they will be able to tolerate a modest increase in food prices to make farming a profitable activity for those people still engaged in it.

But certainly if this degree of concentration of agricultural production ever came about, farm life as we have known or imagined it in our history would disappear. Former Texas commissioner of agriculture Jim Hightower has said, "It comes down to one key question: Are we going to have a system of hardworking, efficient, independent family farmers in this country, or are we going to turn control of our food supply over to a handful of conglomerates and super-farm combines?" Judith L. Woodward, writing in the April 1985 issue of *The Christian Century,* said that "government decisions made in the near future might determine whether the United States continues in the Jeffersonian pattern of family-owned farms or moves toward the South American pattern of landed gentry (or corporations) controlling most of the nation's agriculture."

In recent years, environmentalists have expressed concern about the long-term effects of intensive industrialized agriculture, the concentration of ownership in food production, and the factory-style farming that results. They point, first of all, to an agricultural system that is dependent on petrochemicals, which will become more expensive as world oil reserves decline in the twenty-first century. How efficient can modern farming be if it is so dependent on large inputs of energy and natural resources? Between 1945 and 1970, corn yields rose by 135 percent per acre, but during the same period American farmers increased their use of electricity by 870 percent per acre, their use of fertilizers by more than 1,100 percent per acre, and insecticides by 1,000 percent per acre.

Environmentalists also point to the more than 3 billion tons of irreplaceable topsoil lost every year in the United States through erosion caused by highly mechanized farming, to the poisoning of rivers, lakes, and underground aquifers by agricultural runoff—the mix of fertilizers, pesticides, and other chemicals washed out of the soil by rain—and to the salinization and ruin of other soil by excessive irrigation.

There is also concern about what will happen to the quality of our food under a factory-farming system. With breakthroughs in genetic engineering, crops can be "designed" for ease of harvesting and shipping rather than for nutritional value. Larger farms using mechanized methods and uniform seed varieties discourage genetic diversity among food plants and make them more vulnerable to diseases and future climate changes. In 1970 southern corn leaf blight destroyed 700 million bushels (almost 247 million hl) of corn, or 15 percent of the American crop. This fungus had no trouble racing through large fields planted to one vulnerable species of hybrid corn. Large petrochemical firms have been buying up seed companies and hybridization laboratories, taking control of many genetic patents in the process. Passage of the Plant Variety Protection Act in 1970 has allowed private companies to gain legal patent protection for the hybrid seeds they develop. Among the major owners of seed companies and seed laboratories are oil, chemical, and pharmaceutical firms such as Ciba-Geigy, Royal Dutch Shell, Sandoz, Dekalb-Pfizer, Upjohn, Olin, Celanese, Monsanto, and Occidental Petroleum. It would be reasonable to expect such firms to develop and market plant varieties that require more fertilizers, pesticides, and chemical growth regulators, whether or not that is in the best interests of farmers and consumers. Furthermore, 45,000 Americans, many of them farmers, are treated for pesticide poisoning each year.

Modern agribusiness production methods also trouble environmentalists. In modern feedlots thousands of head of cattle are crowded into small, enclosed areas and given feed according to formulas monitored by computer. Virtually all egg-laying hens, chickens for broiling, and veal calves, and about half of all pigs are now raised in "confinement houses," where they are locked into small cages in large sheds and raised under artificial light. When animals are crowded together like this, disease spreads more rapidly, so cattle and poultry producers add large amounts of antibiotics to their animal feed. Almost half of the antibiotics produced in the United States are used as additives for livestock feed. This has health implications for the humans who consume the meat from such animals: continuous exposure to these antibiotics will lessen their usefulness in fighting disease.

Today more than half of all the food Americans consume is not farm fresh. Instead, it is prepared by about 22,000 food processing operations, where thousands of food colorings, chemical preservatives, flavor enhancers, and nutritional supplements are added and where farm products are mechanically and chemically transformed into new forms. Many urban consumers have never tasted a really fresh vegetable, and others have become addicted to the enhanced flavoring or high sugar content of processed foods. During food processing, much of the nutritional content of food is removed, and the processing itself changes the way we digest it. Health authorities can point to increases in diet-related diseases as a result of eating processed foods, and new industries producing vitamin supplements and health foods have arisen to "fix" our diets. Because of a consumer prejudice against yellow flour, for example, the protein-rich endosperm of the wheat kernel is removed before milling. This process raises the cost of the nutritionally poorer flour and the baked goods made from it. The wheat germ removed from the flour is then sold back to consumers as a dietary supplement in health food stores.

For all these reasons, defenders of federal subsidies to farmers do not believe that agriculture should be allowed to operate under free-market conditions or that we should risk further concentration of ownership in our food production system. Agriculture, they believe, must be viewed not as a business but as a kind of public utility, and the government must have a farm policy just as it has a defense policy. Whatever failures and abuses the farm program has suffered, it has helped the nation to maintain a productive agricultural base, provided Americans with abundant and inexpensive food, and guaranteed a minimum standard of living to many farm families who are unwilling to abandon the traditions of rural life. Heather Ball and Leland Beatty wrote in the November 1984 issue of *The Nation*, "If agriculture were an industry that had resisted innovation and showed declining productivity, perhaps an argument could be made for allowing uncontrolled market forces to clear out the deadwood. But America's decentralized, commercial family farm system is the most successful in the world." In 1986 the Domestic Policy Association concluded that "the best way to sustain agricultural production is to provide a stable market, even if that means paying subsidies to farmers who are not economically distressed. . . . Agriculture needs a moderating hand to smooth out cycles that otherwise would destroy even the best farmers."

Nonsense, say the critics of the farm program. Sixty years of government attempts to exercise a "moderating hand" have not saved millions of farmers. If American farmers are the most successful in the world, we should put an end to artificially high grain prices and allow our farmers to compete effectively in world markets; we should let our agricultural surpluses feed the world. But if we have learned anything in the last two decades, it is that the export market is highly unstable.

The United States now exports more than 50 percent of its wheat and cotton, almost 50 percent of its soybeans, and more than 30 percent of its corn. Selling farm products abroad in the future will present both opportunities and risks. Lester Brown of the Worldwatch Institute predicts vast new demand for agricultural products in China and India as a result of industrialization and population growth. Countries like China and Japan have a relatively small amount of arable land, and Brown believes that food imports will become essential for these countries. Japan, incidentally, in spite of its protectionist policies, must import 90 percent of its food grains and is today the largest market for American farm exports.

On the other hand, the American farmer may face stiff new competition in international markets. Agricultural productivity in the countries of the European Community is increasing. Yields of wheat alone increased by 20 percent in Europe during the 1980s. China, at least in the short run, has not become a major importer of food and has in fact started to export corn and cotton. With the recent approval of the new General Agreement on Tariffs and Trade (GATT), greater quantities of cheap Canadian wheat are already entering American markets.

A number of Third World nations are also increasing their farm output as a result of green revolution hybrid seeds and better techniques. In these developing nations, American exports are not always appreciated. The dumping of American grain into a poor agrarian society can drive down prices and wipe out many local farmers, destroying the efforts of these countries to become self-sufficient in food production. The dream of economists to have the American farmer feed the world may be seen by other nations as a kind of "food imperialism." Whatever the future, it is clear that the export market is another factor that is out of farmers' control, and it will inevitably present them with some surprises.

Federal subsidies to farmers are very expensive and don't seem to help them very much, but elimination of subsidies could be catastrophic for hundreds of thousands of farmers and could change the whole character of American farming. Are there any other alternatives for the future? New, mandatory acreage-reduction programs have been proposed, programs that require the idling of so much acreage that surpluses must disappear and farm prices must rise, making price supports unnecessary. Acreage restrictions do play a role in soil conservation, but this idea has many drawbacks. Historically it has been difficult to enforce and has not worked in the long run. It means more government management of farmers, and it will damage farm supply businesses. For many farmers, the reduced output will be so severe that no increase in farm prices will compensate for the reduced volume. These farmers will suffer a loss of income, and such a massive acreage reduction program will surely bankrupt many of them.

Another suggestion has been to accept that there will be a loss of some farms in the future, but to encourage the remaining farmers to form cooperatives for the marketing of their products. The basic idea behind a cooperative is that a group of farmers agree not to compete and not to sell until the price offered reaches a certain level. A nationwide system of regional cooperatives might succeed in moderating production; if not, at least it would give farmers collective bargaining power in negotiating fairer prices. Again, if farm prices rise high enough, price supports will become unnecessary. This idea has merit, and many successful regional cooperatives are in existence already. But the cooperative movement faces many obstacles. Farmers, though close to one another in their respective communities, are natural competitors and independent thinkers. Not all farms or farm organizations share the same interests. Small farms and large farms face different problems. The corn farmer wants high prices for feed grains; the cattle or poultry farmer wants feed-grain prices to be low. Farmers simply have a lot of difficulty working in concert. And cooperatives have not fared well against the agribusiness system, which is much larger, more complex, and more powerful than it was when cooperatives first fought for independence in the late nineteenth century.

All of the various proposals calling for acreage reduction or cooperative marketing involve attempts to regulate the amount of farm products reaching the market, either by reducing farm output directly or by having farmers withhold their harvests until prices are bid up. These strategies require some government management and will lead to higher food prices. Those who suggest ending price supports and returning to the free market say that if international trade barriers disappear and if the export market remains strong, their solution will make it unnecessary to interfere with farm production in any way or to adopt an essentially irrational plan of restricting the world's supply of food. The "invisible hand" of the market, the collective decisions of buyers and sellers, must decide how many farmers produce how much food.

Most of the nation's farms are still family-owned. Ownership and management of farmland seem to be a financial nightmare that even corporations involved in the food business would rather avoid. More than that, there is a connection between dependence on the limited resources of family labor and the need to continually apply new techniques to make that labor more efficient and competitive. The dollar investment in capital—machinery and equipment—is twice as great for a farmworker as it is for a non-farmworker. Family farm labor has been the key to advances in agricultural technology and the reason why American farmers are so productive. But now economists tell us that the age of the yeoman farmer is over, that mechanized commercial superfarms are more efficient, and that whatever role family farmers may have played in the past, they have produced themselves out of a job.

The 98 percent of Americans who are not farmers, but who hold the political power to decide the fate of the farm sector, will have to make some hard choices in the future. Do we want to maintain a large and diverse population of competitive family farmers working their own land, supporting prosperous rural communities, producing a cheap and abundant supply of food? If so, are we willing to pay the cost in taxes for federal programs to keep a large number of uneconomic farming units in business? Are we willing to deny ourselves and the rest of the world the full benefits of advancing agricultural technology and pay for schemes that would restrict farm output? Or should we save ourselves the tax bill, end the farm program, and allow the natural evolution of a free market economy to determine the number and types of farms and the nature of our farm production system? If so, are we willing to accept higher food prices? Economists suggest that such price increases will average no more than 5 or 6 percent because farm prices are really a very small part of retail food prices. But that is not true of meat and poultry products, where feed grain represents a significant cost to producers. Remember that in 1973, when the Soviets made their massive grain purchases and cleared out the surpluses, food prices in the United States rose by 20 percent. And can we live with the social and environmental costs of the large-scale, high-tech, fully integrated commercial farming system that may evolve?

There are no easy answers. As Lauren Soth says in *An Embarassment of Plenty*, "Farm programs designed to keep commercial agriculture healthy, to keep food costs low, and to stimulate technical advances are poorly designed to meet the problems of poverty in agriculture." Any alternative program to increase farm prosperity within a free market economy will ultimately reduce the number of people in farming and raise food prices. The choice we make will determine whether or not the family farmer survives, what type of food production system evolves in the United States, and what kind of food will be placed on American tables in the decades to come.

FOR FURTHER READING

Belden, Joseph N. *Dirt Rich, Dirt Poor: America's Food and Farm Crisis.* New York: Routledge & Kegan Paul, 1986.

Bird, Alan R. *Surplus . . . The Riddle of American Agriculture.* New York: Springer, 1962.

Bovard, James. *The Farm Fiasco.* San Francisco: Institute for Contemporary Studies, 1991.

Burbach, Roger, and Patricia Flynn. *Agribusiness in the Americas.* New York: Monthly Review Press, 1980.

Cherrington, Mark. *Degradation of the Land.* New York: Chelsea House, 1992.

Doyle, Jack. *Altered Harvest.* New York: Viking Penguin, 1985.

Edwin, Ed. *Feast or Famine: Food, Farming, and Farm Politics in America.* New York: Charterhouse, 1974.

Fowler, Cary, and Pat Mooney. *Shattering: Food, Politics, and the Loss of Genetic Diversity.* Tucson: University of Arizona Press, 1990.

Fox, Michael W. *Agricide.* New York: Schocken Books, 1986.

Hart, John Fraser. *The Land That Feeds Us.* New York: Norton, 1991.

Heiser, Charles B., Jr. *Seed to Civilization: The Story of Man's Food.* San Francisco: Freeman, 1973.

Howard, Robert West. *The Vanishing Land.* New York: Villard Books, 1985.

Long, Robert Emmet, ed. *The Farm Crisis.* New York: Wilson, 1987.

McElvaine, Robert S. *The Great Depression.* New York: Times Books, 1984.

Morgan, Dan. *Merchants of Grain.* New York: Viking Press, 1979.

Paulsen, Gary. *Farm: A History and Celebration of the American Farmer.* Englewood Cliffs, N.J.: Prentice-Hall, 1977.

Rapp, David. *How the U.S. Got into Agriculture and Why It Can't Get Out.* Washington, D.C.: Congressional Quarterly, 1988.

Ritchie, Carson I. A. *Food in Civilization.* New York: Beaufort Books, 1981.

Solkoff, Joel. *The Politics of Food.* San Francisco: Sierra Club Books, 1985.

Soth, Lauren. *An Embarassment of Plenty.* New York: Crowell, 1965.

INDEX

(Page numbers in *italic* refer to illustrations.)

127